L**in**ked *TO* INFLUENCE

7 POWERFUL RULES FOR BECOMING A TOP INFLUENCER IN YOUR MARKET AND ATTRACTING YOUR IDEAL CLIENTS ON LINKEDIN

D0569330

BY: STEPHANIE SAMMONS

StephanieSammons.com

Publishing services provided by  Archangel Ink

ISBN: 1942761708
ISBN-13: 978-1-942761-70-9

This book is dedicated to Mike Stelzner, founder of
SocialMediaExaminer.com and the Social Media Marketing World
Conference. Thank you for giving me a multitude of opportunities to grow
my influence and for pushing me to be better.

Table of Contents

Introduction

In June 2009, I quit my job. I walked away from a fifteen-year corporate financial services career to pursue my dream of becoming an entrepreneur. I wasn't exactly prepared for this move, nor did I anticipate the major identity crisis that would accompany it. But I knew deep down that I had to do something different with my life. Ultimately, I no longer had any real job security, and I was not in control of my destiny. It was time to go.

Although it was a terrible time for a career change (on the heels of the major financial crisis), it ended up being the best move I have ever made. The timing of my departure coincided with the emergence of social networking platforms like LinkedIn, which were quickly changing the way we connect and do business.

LinkedIn had been around for a few years, but I had never paid much attention. My company restricted the use of online social networking due to regulations. As a new entrepreneur, I was free to explore. I slowly began to dive into LinkedIn to learn more about the business-networking opportunities.

LinkedIn ended up saving my life. I needed an effective way to quickly seek out people, ideas, and resources that could help me launch and grow my marketing consulting business. LinkedIn was the answer for me.

I don't recommend waiting to leverage LinkedIn until you need it, like I did. Instead, start building your presence before you ever need help. You never know what curveballs life is going to throw you, especially in this day and age.

While I was learning how to master LinkedIn, I saw many of my digital marketing peers focusing on other platforms like Facebook and Twitter. They tended to be less excited about the potential of LinkedIn. But I stuck with LinkedIn, because I knew that access to this vast database of businesspeople and content was extremely valuable (if I could figure out how to effectively tap into it).

It certainly wasn't my intention to become a teacher of LinkedIn. However, I am a teacher and a coach at heart. I spent my first couple of years out of college as a high school business teacher and girls' basketball coach. Teaching has always been a core part of my business experience working with clients.

The more I understood the value of LinkedIn as a business tool, the more I wanted to share this knowledge with my clients and community. I began writing and speaking about my LinkedIn insights and strategies for entrepreneurs and professionals. When you speak on a topic, you have very little time to go into great detail in your presentation. This book allows me the freedom to share in-depth knowledge with you. Essentially, this book is a comprehensive LinkedIn marketing playbook.

My LinkedIn marketing methodology is different than that of most of the experts' out there. I take a more strategic, patient approach. I come from the school of employing "trust-based" marketing for developing long-term (and loyal) client or customer relationships. This method of marketing is designed to build your personal influence. The more influence you build, the more attractive you become to your ideal clients.

As a financial advisor, I had to *earn* the trust and respect of my wealthy, retiring clients. I had to guide, influence, and serve these individuals for months, and in some cases years, before they made the decision to work with me.

I learned that landing a new client wasn't so great if that person was someone you didn't enjoy working with. Finding ideal clients became my mission. Who wants to build a business where you work with a bunch of clients you don't really enjoy?

My LinkedIn marketing strategy is designed to help you become more influential and to grow your business with your *ideal* clients in the process. It is grounded in building trust with anyone and everyone who matters to your business. For me, there is no other way to protect your reputation and attract the best client relationships.

The great advantage of LinkedIn is that you can *accelerate* the trust-building process like never before. You have access to information about people and avenues to connect with them that were not previously available.

With LinkedIn, you can literally *see* beyond your 1st-degree network and gain exposure to your extended network, which has never been possible before. And you can provide value by sharing your ideas and insights. I believe that LinkedIn represents one of the greatest business-building opportunities in history, especially if your business depends on relationships and referrals.

With this book, my goal is to serve as your instructor. I will teach you my proven process for building personal influence on LinkedIn, so that you can start attracting ideal clients and opportunities to your business.

The book consists of **seven powerful rules**. These rules are meant to serve as strategic *guideposts* for you to follow. They will give you a framework for understanding and leveraging the most important tools that LinkedIn has to offer you.

I am excited to share my process with you and help you take your LinkedIn presence (and your business) to the next level. I want these words to truly make a difference in your business and in your life. Thank you for giving me this opportunity to share my ideas and insights with you. I hope you find them to be valuable.

To help you follow along and think more clearly about your LinkedIn strategy, I have created a complementary mini PDF workbook for you. You can download your workbook by visiting this page on my website: www.stephaniesammons.com/linked-to-influence-workbook

The LinkedIn Opportunity

L inkedIn is the most powerful business-networking resource in history. It is a global, virtual, perpetual networking event! LinkedIn is currently the best professional platform for growing your personal influence, building a loyal referral network, positioning yourself as a thought leader, and attracting your ideal clients.

At the time of this writing, LinkedIn is quickly approaching 400 million members worldwide. One in every three professionals is an official LinkedIn member. LinkedIn members view the platform as a valuable, trusted destination for growing their networks, uncovering job and business opportunities, and gathering professional and industry insights.

LinkedIn members are also active, educated, and affluent. Over 40 percent of members earn $100,000 or more per year and 60 percent earn more than $75,000 per year. LinkedIn members are businesspeople, and a good majority of them are the decision-makers!

Having access to a *trusted,* professional platform where you can accelerate the growth of your influence and network is a game changer for those who take advantage. If you are an entrepreneur or business professional in the digital age, LinkedIn is a no-brainer opportunity for growing your business.

Do You Need a Premium LinkedIn Account?

A question I am frequently asked about LinkedIn is, "Should I sign up for a premium account?"

My general answer to this question is YES. If you are serious about tapping into all that LinkedIn has to offer and you can afford to upgrade, do so. The additional benefits of a premium account are quite valuable, especially with regard to one-to-one communication and LinkedIn search tools.

Over time, LinkedIn has continued to take away some of the benefits that were available previously with a free account. That doesn't mean a free account is worthless. There are still plenty of benefits if you do stick with a free account.

A premium LinkedIn account includes benefits such as enhanced searches (more results and filters) and InMails (the ability to send messages to any LinkedIn member, even if you're not connected). Premium members gain greater visibility on LinkedIn and access to more profile data.

There are several premium account options and pricing levels to choose from. You will save money if you pay on an annual basis. You can also upgrade or downgrade your account at any time.

A premium LinkedIn account has exposed me to invaluable connections, business opportunities, and insights. You will have to make your own decision about whether it makes sense for you to upgrade your account.

Making the LinkedIn Commitment

Whether you decide on a premium account doesn't matter nearly as much as making the commitment to developing and growing your LinkedIn presence.

You can leapfrog your competitors by applying what you learn in this book. You will learn strategies and tactics that, without a doubt, will separate you from your competitors. I can't guarantee results for you, but I can tell you that if you consistently implement what you learn in this book, you will become more influential in your industry, market, or niche, and good things will happen for your business.

You may have noticed that the title of this book is *Linked to Influence*. Let me share with you why I believe building your personal influence on LinkedIn (and across the social web) is so critical for attracting your ideal clients and customers today.

Linked to Influence

One of the most powerful ways to grow your business in today's digital age is to build your personal influence. Building personal influence isn't about marketing your products or services. It's about marketing your *message* in a way that provides significant value to your ideal clients or customers.

Influence is no longer limited to the elite few. As my friend, Mark Schaefer, says in his book *Return on Influence*, "Influence has been democratized." Mark is correct. YOU can establish yourself as an influencer, starting right now!

You can become that credible, sought-after expert and work exclusively with the clients (and/or customers) you want to work with in the way you want to work with them. It sounds appealing, doesn't it? With the ability to create a powerful online presence through access to social networks like LinkedIn, it is very achievable.

To build personal influence, you don't have to wait for someone to choose you or give you permission.

Influence is the New Authority

Being viewed as an "authority" is no longer enough in today's democratized, digital society. Certainly you need to know your stuff and be competent at what you do. That's a given. But you need more than expertise and experience to attract your ideal clients. You need *influence*. Influence extends beyond authority.

We follow and work with influencers because of who they are, what they know, what they believe, and how they think. They strike a chord with us and make us feel inspired. They lead us. They motivate and empower us.

Think about the people who have influenced you. Why do you follow them? What have they done for you? How have they impacted your life?

Trusted influencers are leaders in their respective industries, markets, and niches. They have impeccable reputations and operate with integrity. Influencers do not try to help everyone. They know exactly whom they can help. Influencers are laser focused on serving their ideal clients or customers.

People admire, trust, and respect influencers. They seek the advice and guidance of influencers. People want to learn from and work with influencers because of *who* they are, and people are willing to pay for that privilege.

When you build your personal influence, your digital activities will have a much greater impact, and you will spend less time and energy to achieve the same results!

How Do You Build Personal Influence Today?

Building your personal influence on LinkedIn (and online in general) is a process. It doesn't happen overnight—it accumulates over time. Influence is like an investment portfolio where you keep adding to it consistently until you have a substantial nest egg that will pay you dividends and interest for the rest of your professional life!

First, to build your personal influence, you need to be more *personable* online. Show your personality and share personal insights and stories that your ideal clients can relate to. Can you do this on LinkedIn? Absolutely.

Creating a more *personalized* professional brand through your LinkedIn presence is something I strongly recommend. I'll talk more about this in Rule #1.

Next, you need to consistently share your *perspective*. It's not enough to share what you know. You also need to share what you think! It is your unique *message* that you want to market in a way that adds significant value to your ideal clients, not your products and services.

Last, but certainly not least, you need to add *real value* to the lives of your ideal clients or customers. You need to give away knowledge, insights, and guidance that can change their lives for the better.

With so much information available online now, it is very difficult for most people to synthesize and process it all. By doing this work for your ideal clients and customers while infusing it with your own personality and perspective, you will be viewed as a trusted influencer.

When you build your personal influence, your business will grow automatically and exponentially.

Personal Influence and LinkedIn Go Hand in Hand

LinkedIn provides an incredible opportunity to build your personal influence.

Everything you do on LinkedIn is tied to your *personal* LinkedIn profile. You have opportunities to build your personal influence on LinkedIn through your profile, your networking activities, group discussions, one-to-one contact, content sharing, content publishing, and more.

Throughout this book, you will see that this personal-influence concept I'm so crazy about serves as the underlying foundation to everything I teach about LinkedIn.

Just remember this: if you focus on building your personal influence on LinkedIn, it will *compound* your results.

Hopefully you have a better understanding about why I'm such a fan of building personal influence. That's truly how you get *Linked to Influence*. Now, let's move on to the seven rules for becoming a top influencer in your market and attracting your ideal clients on LinkedIn! Are you ready? Turn the page!

Chapter 1

RULE #1—Power Up Your Profile (with Precision)

> *Whenever you do a thing, act as if all the world were watching.*
>
> - Thomas Jefferson

A neurosurgeon is very precise when operating on a patient. Using the exact medical procedure and surgical tools required, the neurosurgeon operates on the patient's specific problem.

Do you operate with this level of precision in your business? Do you have a targeted message and method to address a specific problem with your ideal clients or customers?

Your LinkedIn profile serves as your surgical tool for attracting the right people and opportunities to your business. Your profile should include *precise* information that is designed to specifically appeal to that exact prospective client you are looking to work with.

You don't have to be a neurosurgeon, but if you want to leverage your LinkedIn profile to grow your business, power it up with *precision*.

Your LinkedIn Profile = Your Professional Identity

Your LinkedIn profile is, by default, your new professional identity. Whether you are prepared for it or not, it is likely that hundreds, if not thousands of people are going to stumble across your LinkedIn profile. Some of these individuals undoubtedly will be your ideal clients. These are the people you want to be prepared for!

Your LinkedIn profile is also the gateway to growing your professional network and building your personal influence. It is the center of your LinkedIn presence.

Just claiming your LinkedIn profile and completing the basics is not enough. You need to create a strategic, compelling, and optimized LinkedIn profile in order to stand out and attract your ideal clients and customers.

10 Reasons Your LinkedIn Profile Matters for Business

I'm amazed at how many people view their LinkedIn profile as an online resume. Yikes! Please don't do this. Your LinkedIn profile is a client-attraction center. You should value it as such!

Like a resume, your LinkedIn profile can show off your past and current work experience and education, but it is much more than that. It is one of the most valuable social media assets you can invest your time and energy into building and improving.

There is no other social media profile that gives you as much space and capability to showcase who you are, who you help, how you help, and what you've accomplished in your professional career.

Here are ten reasons your LinkedIn profile is important:

1) Your profile serves as your default, online professional identity. As Facebook is to your personal life, LinkedIn is to your professional life.

2) Your profile is tied to all of your LinkedIn activity. Fro networking to group participation to publishing, it follows you everywhere.
3) Your profile is discoverable within and outside of LinkedIn. It can be found in Google searches, for example.
4) Your profile is a frontline connection tool. Many times, it's going to be the first experience that a potential client or referral source will have with you.
5) Your profile is a one-page digital summary that can tell your story and share your message efficiently and effectively.
6) Your profile serves as a hub for your thought leadership. When you publish articles on LinkedIn's Publishing Platform, your most recent posts are displayed prominently on your profile.
7) Your profile is a showcase for your rich media assets (such as videos, podcasts, and presentations) that enable you to create a more human connection and accelerate the relationship-building process.
8) Your profile displays the professional timeline of your education, experience, and accomplishments. Viewers can see where you've been and what you've done in your career.
9) Your profile is a conduit for driving traffic to your website and/or specific landing pages for lead generation.
10) Your profile is a *social proof* builder. Viewers of your profile can see endorsements of your skills and recommendations of your work by others.

Professionally "Personalize" Your LinkedIn Profile

There are opportunities throughout your profile for branding YOU. Why would you want to do this?

Ultimately, it is your personal brand that differentiates you from everyone else in your market. No one can be you.

Remember, business is personal. People do business with people. Your LinkedIn profile provides an opportunity for you to connect on a personal level with your ideal clients or customers.

The fact that all LinkedIn profiles look alike means that it is the words, images, and media you use to tell your story that create the difference.

I have three Ps for you to utilize to make your profile more personalized. Showcasing your *personality*, your *passion* for what you do, and your unique *perspective* throughout your LinkedIn profile will make you more human, magnetic, memorable, and influential.

I'll talk more about these three Ps and how to use them later in the book.

A Personalized LinkedIn Profile Can Break Through the Digital Barrier

As I recently sat in the office of a prospective client, I reflected upon what I had learned about him online. We were connected on LinkedIn and the other big social networks. Because of this, I had gathered plenty of information about him, and I thought I had a pretty good idea of what he would be like in person.

Sitting face-to-face with him completely changed my perception. There was so much more depth and personality to this prospective client than I had ever been able to experience online. His social media presence just didn't do him justice.

This is when I first became aware that there can be a *significant* gap between who you appear to be online and how you are in real life.

I call this the *digital barrier.* The only way to minimize the gap (you can't close it completely unless you are face-to-face) is to *personalize* your online presence, and that includes your LinkedIn profile.

This is one of the reasons why podcast (audio) and video content are so valuable today. They have the ability to reduce the digital barrier.

Fortunately, you can infuse these rich media assets into your LinkedIn profile and show a much more realistic view of who you are and what it might be like to interact with you in person!

Understanding the Value of Profile Views

Before we get into how to build a powerful and precise LinkedIn profile, I want you to better understand how important **profile views** are.

The number of profile views you receive is a function of the content in your LinkedIn profile, your LinkedIn network, and your LinkedIn activity.

Profile views lead to great things like more relevant connections, engagement, website visits, speaking opportunities, media inquiries, partnerships, and new prospects, clients, referrals, and team members.

One of the most popular LinkedIn features is the "Who's Viewed Your Profile" feature. You can see who has viewed your profile as long as they have made their details visible.

Once someone has viewed your profile, you have the perfect opportunity to reach out and connect. This can also work in the reverse. When you view profiles on LinkedIn, you will naturally stir up the curiosity of the individual you viewed. They may reach out to you to connect.

In the "Who's Viewed Your Profile" area of your LinkedIn account, you will see the number of profile views you have received, including ninety days' worth of trends. You can also see who specifically has viewed your profile. (If you have a premium

LinkedIn account, you have access to more data about who is viewing your profile.)

LinkedIn also shows you where your profile ranks among your connections, as well as other professionals on LinkedIn who are similar to you. It's human nature to want to get to the top of those rankings, but they mean nothing if the viewers of your profile are not relevant.

A quality LinkedIn network will generate more relevant people viewing your profile. You attract a more quality network by being as *precise* as possible with your profile content!

What I like best about this data is that LinkedIn makes proactive suggestions for actions you can take to increase your profile views, such as following companies and joining certain groups.

Some of your profile views will come from passive sources such as LinkedIn and Google searches, and many of your views will fall into the "other" and "unknown" categories. This could be the case if you are speaking at an event, for example, and ask that the audience connect with you on LinkedIn.

There is a direct correlation between how active you are on LinkedIn and the number of profile views you receive. Your LinkedIn activity drives your profile visibility. If your activity is *precisely* geared toward adding value to your ideal clients or customers, you are going to get more profile views from these individuals!

The Role of Your LinkedIn Profile in Driving Referrals

Asking for referrals is an uncomfortable thing to do, isn't it? I have always hated doing this. It doesn't matter how you frame it, asking someone to refer you business just feels desperate and pushy.

If you do a nice job with your LinkedIn profile, you set yourself up for attracting and earning referrals without having to ask for them. Let me explain.

A trusted contact who feels confident in your LinkedIn profile is not going to hesitate to make an introduction or refer you to a friend. The more you appear to know what you are doing on LinkedIn, the more referrals like this you can receive. It is very simple for someone to send a friend the link to your profile to make a referral. It requires very little effort today.

A prospective client who has been referred to you should also be able to view your LinkedIn profile and be very clear on what you do, exactly who you help, and how or why you are different. (Remember, that "difference" factor will really come through when you showcase the three Ps [your personality, passion, and perspective].)

Another conversation that takes place frequently within LinkedIn, both publicly and privately, is members asking their connections: **Who do you know or who can you recommend to help me with "fill in the blank?"**

With your LinkedIn profile, the more precise you are about who you help and how you help, the more your network connections will know who would be a good client for you. You need to teach them through the language you use in your profile.

It's also important to realize that your LinkedIn profile may not serve as the beginning or the end point for a referral relationship, but it can play a significant role in the process. Your LinkedIn profile can support the referral process and move it forward.

Recently I received a referral from one of my LinkedIn connections. I noticed that she had viewed my LinkedIn profile prior to reaching out. A few days later, she referred a potential client to me.

It was my LinkedIn profile that facilitated the referral and established immediate credibility with the prospective client. She was most of the way through her decision to work with me before we ever spoke on the phone.

Understand that your LinkedIn profile is creating an *ongoing* first impression. It can establish your credibility and accelerate the relationship-building process before you ever engage.

The Importance of Completing Your Profile

LinkedIn says that *members who have a complete profile are forty times more likely to receive opportunities*. The top level of profile completion is "All-Star." If your profile isn't All-Star status, you will want to get it there. The way you achieve All-Star status is simple: **complete your profile**.

I recommend completing as many sections as possible on your LinkedIn profile. LinkedIn views a completed profile as including your industry, location, current position with description, two past positions, education, skills (at least three), a profile photo, and fifty connections.

There are a couple of important benefits to having a completed LinkedIn profile. First, a complete profile is going to make a much better impression on your viewers than one that is missing a picture or work experience, which could suggest you are hiding something.

Second, a complete LinkedIn profile will likely show up higher in LinkedIn search results. Search results are tied to relevancy to such things as common connections; connections by 1st, 2nd, and 3rd degree; and common groups. If you don't have a complete LinkedIn profile, you may not show up at all in search results!

Remember, you want to be as precise as possible with the information and content you put into your LinkedIn profile. Gear it toward the ideal clients and customers you want to attract. Use their words and empathize with their top concern or problem that you have the solution for.

Stuffing your LinkedIn profile with irrelevant information just to fill it up will not serve you nearly, as well as being precise. In the sections to follow, keep this concept of *precision* in mind as I walk you through the development of each part of your profile.

Put Your Best Face Forward

A compelling LinkedIn profile starts with putting your best face forward. There is nothing more personal than your face! Your LinkedIn profile picture can honestly make you or break you, especially with a first impression.

A compelling profile picture will speak volumes about your level of professionalism and potentially spark an immediate human connection.

Your LinkedIn profile picture follows you everywhere on LinkedIn (along with your headline statement). This part of your profile should not be the default LinkedIn avatar (no picture), an outdated headshot, a selfie, a full-body image, or a snapshot where you've cropped your face out! And no pets!

Your profile picture should be a current, professional, and friendly headshot. It's all about putting your best face forward for that potential client or customer you have yet to meet!

Here are some recommendations for making the most of your LinkedIn profile picture:

- **Hire a professional photographer.** This is your professional image! There are many affordable photographers out there who can take your picture. It doesn't have to be fancy, but it does need to be professional.

- **Smile.** There was a time when I had a LinkedIn profile picture where I looked a bit intense. I received some feedback on this picture from a trusted colleague who said, "Where is your smile?" I realized that this particular headshot made me seem less approachable. I removed it and replaced it with a picture of me smiling. What a difference a smile can make. Although looking serious might be your style, ask others who know you well if it's a good look for you.

- **Look straight ahead.** I get some pushback on this one from time to time, but I think it's important to show your eyes in your profile picture! When you meet someone new you don't look off to the side or down at the ground, do you? These types of headshots are common, and they may work very well on a website. For building trust, however, looking straight ahead with your eyes up works best for your LinkedIn profile picture.

- **Update your image.** It's time to get rid of that old headshot from ten years ago. I recommend updating your profile picture every couple of years. Think about it this way—when you meet a LinkedIn connection in person, you want them to be able to recognize you immediately.

- **Upload a background image to your profile.** The background image at the top of your profile is one of the best ways to add some personalization. I recommend creating a professional image to upload here. The background image dimensions are 1400 x 425.

You can use a tool like Canva.com to create your own background image, or you can always hire someone from Fiverr.com to do this for you at a very low cost. Or, you could choose one of the images LinkedIn provides. Just remember that this area is valuable real estate for reinforcing your professionalism and your personal brand.

Craft a Compelling Headline Statement

If your profile picture is the most important component of your LinkedIn profile, your *headline statement* is next in line.

Your LinkedIn headline statement sits at the top of your profile next to your picture. Like your picture, it also follows you across LinkedIn. Your headline statement can serve as an important client-attraction tool. The words you use here can determine whether or not someone clicks through to view your entire profile.

For your profile headline statement, you have 120 characters to work with. Every word you include in your headline statement can have an impact on how you are found on LinkedIn. Ideally, you want to optimize your headline statement using *precise* short phrases or keywords that appeal to your ideal clients and customers.

I suggest when editing your LinkedIn headline statement or any other part of your profile to set the "Notify your Network" setting to **No**. That way your connections won't be alerted every time you make a change.

Optimize your LinkedIn headline statement by describing *what you are known for (or what you do)* and *whom you serve*.

Are you the founder of a company? Are you an author? Are you an entrepreneur? Are you an attorney or financial advisor? Are there descriptive words you can add to be more specific about what you are known for, such as "Founder of XYZ, Inc.," "Dallas Personal Injury Lawyer," or "Digital Marketing Specialist"?

Creating the "what you are known for" component of your headline statement is important for enhancing your credibility and communicating your expertise.

The next most critical piece of your LinkedIn headline statement is who you specifically serve. Who is your target audience, ideal client, or customer? Without this piece, the assumption is that you serve everyone. When you serve everyone, you serve no one.

Beyond including what you are known for and who you serve in your headline statement, consider adding a personal tidbit if you have the room.

For example, in my LinkedIn headline statement, I say I'm a "Texas Gal." This is something that differentiates me. Most people think Texans are friendly and approachable (and of course we are)!

Sallie Krawcheck, the past CEO of Merrill Lynch and now the Chair of Ellevate Network, includes that she is a "crazed UNC basketball fan" in her headline statement. Here is a high-level executive sharing a personal tidbit in her profile headline!

The point is, when you include a personal tidbit in your headline statement, you become more personable.

The words you use in your LinkedIn headline statement can impact how you show up in LinkedIn searches. LinkedIn may also showcase your profile in the sidebar of profiles that are similar to yours. (If you do not want people similar to you to be showcased on your profile, you can disable it in your settings.)

Don't be afraid to experiment with your headline statement and change it up from time to time. As your business or career path evolves, your LinkedIn headline description will need to be updated. You may also find that a new statement performs better in terms of profile views and new connections.

When I added the word "Author" to my headline statement, I noticed new profile views from LinkedIn members who work for various media outlets and book publishers.

Make sure to check out the "Who's Viewed Your Profile" section on LinkedIn to gain specific insights into how you are getting found on LinkedIn and who is viewing your profile. This data is invaluable for optimizing your headline statement for relevant discovery.

Use Keywords in Your Profile Where They Count

Keywords are words or phrases that your ideal clients or customers might use to search for you using LinkedIn's internal search tool.

There are a number of places where descriptive keywords are recognized in your LinkedIn profile. Many LinkedIn experts place a big emphasis on strategically inserting keywords throughout your LinkedIn profile, and for good reason. Keywords can help you get found in LinkedIn searches.

Certainly some of your new connections will come from LinkedIn searches. However, if you are doing a good job in building your personal influence on LinkedIn, and you focus on building a smarter network (Rule #2), you really don't have to worry too much about keywords.

The more influential you become in your market, niche, or industry, the more you will attract relevant profile views simply because of *who* you are. People will deliberately look for you on LinkedIn! They will seek you out.

Your LinkedIn profile should be written first and foremost to appeal to your ideal clients and customers. Keyword infusion should definitely be an afterthought.

There are three primary sections of your LinkedIn profile where keywords are considered:

1) your headline;
2) your LinkedIn summary; and
3) your current and past work experience.

The skills that you choose to receive endorsements for are also likely to be considered keywords for search purposes.

Keywords are typically one-word to three-word phrases that describe a skill, expertise, or title that you have. Always choose keywords that your clients and customers would use to describe you. Stay away from industry jargon.

Customize Your LinkedIn Profile URL

Customizing your profile URL is a simple but valuable exercise. If possible, you will want to use your full name for your profile URL.

I'm amazed at how many LinkedIn members still haven't customized their profile URLs. You can customize yours when you go in to edit your profile.

For example, my LinkedIn profile URL is: www.linkedin.com/in/stephaniesammons where the "Stephanie Sammons" part of my LinkedIn URL has been customized.

The reason for customizing your profile URL is because no one else can grab your name on LinkedIn and build around your identity. Ideally, your profile URL matches your personal brand.

If your full name is not available, try adding a middle initial or, if possible, you could shorten your first name (I could shorten "Stephanie" to "Steph," for example). If that doesn't work, you will have to use some sort of variation of your name. You could add a title or designation (like "CEO"), or even a number at the end of your name.

If you change your LinkedIn profile URL, make sure you update this link anywhere else it might be listed online! The old link will no longer work once it's updated.

Customize Your Profile Website Link Descriptions

LinkedIn gives you three customizable links for your profile. These links can go to external web pages like your website or blog. Unfortunately, these links aren't as visible as they once were, but they still matter. If someone views your profile and becomes interested in learning more about you, they may click on the link to your website.

You may not realize that you can customize these link descriptions instead of using the default generic terms such as "website" or "blog." Use a short few words to describe the web links, such as the name of your company or blog, or even a special offer you have.

For example, one of my links points to a free guide that I offer and points to a specific landing page for that offer. You could also link to your profile on another social network, or to a social media group that you manage.

Craft a Compelling LinkedIn Summary

Your LinkedIn summary is the centerpiece of your profile. This is where you get to tell your story and share your message. No other social network gives you as much space to do so. You get two thousand characters for your LinkedIn summary, and I recommend using the entire space if possible.

A common question is whether or not to write your LinkedIn summary in the first person or the third person. I'm a big believer in writing it in the first person, as if you are speaking directly to the viewer. This is how you make a personal connection.

When your LinkedIn profile is written in the third person, it comes across as formal and impersonal. This is your opportunity to make a connection and build influence with your ideal clients and customers.

Your LinkedIn profile summary is where profile *precision* matters most. This is the area where you make your ideal clients and customers feel as if you completely understand their situation and that you also have the solution.

Demonstrating that you have the solution is not the same as promoting your products and services in your summary. Do not do this. Simply tell the story of how you have helped others just like them to get from point A to point B.

Right off the bat in your profile summary, you want to get your message out.

Here are three questions to answer that can help you craft your core profile message:

1) What is the specific problem or challenge you help your ideal clients and customers solve?
2) What is your solution (otherwise known as your value)?
3) Who else have you helped in the same situation and how are they better off?

Sharing your core message in your LinkedIn profile summary is vital. But just as important is sharing your story and purpose. I want to spend a little time on this because it is so critical to making a connection with your clients, customers, and community online.

Why do you do what you do?

A lawyer friend of mine lost her mother tragically and unexpectedly as a young adult. She helps families who deal with tragedies like this every day through her work. For most people, dealing with these heavy, emotional situations would be difficult and exhausting. Because of her personal experience, she is well equipped to help others through the legal AND emotional process of dealing with sudden tragedy or loss.

When I encouraged my lawyer friend to share her story publicly, at first she balked. However, I convinced her that her story had incredible power to provide hope to the people she was helping!

By sharing her story publicly, my lawyer friend can facilitate a deeper human connection with her existing and prospective clients. They will know that she truly understands what they are going through.

Your story *fuels* your purpose.

You certainly don't need to go into great detail on your LinkedIn profile (or anywhere else online) about your story, but you should absolutely attempt to weave it into your message.

I had to do some deep thinking about how my story connected to my purpose. You may need to do the same.

I realized that the reason I'm so passionate about guiding others to become more confident in sharing their message on a digital stage is no coincidence. I am drawn to this cause due to my lifelong struggle to be true to myself in the face of judgment and rejection.

How are the two related? What I've found is that many professionals struggle immensely with moving from their *offline* comfort zone onto the great *digital* stage, where judgment and rejection are lurking all around.

They have anxiety about putting their personal story, ideas, and insights out on display for everyone to see. They fear judgment from clients, colleagues, peers, and competitors. They worry about having to be perfect, and they are afraid of being too vulnerable. They don't know what to say and how to say it.

What they do know is that in order to create sustainable success in the digital age, they *must* do this.

Most of us aren't professional writers, filmmakers, performers, or radio personalities by trade. We are brand new at sharing our personalities, passions, and perspectives publicly on a digital stage. We are like insecure teenagers who really want to fit in and be accepted!

I know this struggle all too well. For me, the process of putting myself out there online has been more liberating than most could ever imagine because of my life experience. I understand the downside of suppressing your voice and the power of singing out at the top of your lungs!

My core purpose today is teaching my clients and community members how to confidently share their message on a digital stage to reach their goals in business and in life.

What is your story?

Think about your own story and how it has led you to do what you do today. Think about how you can weave your story into your message, and into your LinkedIn profile summary.

You will be amazed at what sharing your story publicly can do for your own growth, as well as the growth of your business.

Now, on to the rest of your LinkedIn profile summary!

Additional information to consider including in your LinkedIn profile summary:

- An original work you've created (process, course, book, etc.)
- Where someone could learn more about you (insert a full link to your website—this link will only be live on the LinkedIn mobile app)
- Meaningful third-party accolades or accomplishments such as being an author or speaker (if applicable)
- Work history that relates to what you do today
- Personal tidbits about your interests, hobbies, and even family, outside of your work life! (I can't tell you how often this piece of my profile summary has sparked a conversation on LinkedIn.)
- Any chance you have to weave your personality, passion, and perspective into your profile summary, do it!
- To make your profile summary easier to read, break up your paragraphs and try to use shorter sentences.
- Insert the URL to your website in your summary at least once to make it easier for visitors to find you on the web.
- I recommend writing a draft of your LinkedIn summary outside of LinkedIn until you are happy with it. From

there, you can copy and paste it in. There have been many times when editing my profile that it did not save within LinkedIn and I lost the changes.

- Lastly, don't be afraid to make changes and updates to your profile summary. Your story and your message can evolve over time!

How to Showcase Your Work Experience

In order for LinkedIn to consider your profile complete, you need at least one current position and two past positions listed.

If you don't have two past positions, you could add a separate entry for different positions you've held within the same company or even different services you've offered within the same company. For example, a financial advisor could have one position under the same company showcasing financial planning and another showcasing investment management.

Also, if you've done any project or consulting work that wasn't necessarily full time, you could add this as a separate work experience entry. You can also add an entry if you are currently looking for employment!

The work experience seems to trip members up who don't necessarily have two past positions and one present position. Don't let this deter you from completing your profile.

On the other end of the spectrum, I've seen profiles with twenty plus listings under their "Work Experience" section where they've included projects that were perhaps short-term or more freelance oriented. I recommend saving the "Work Experience" section for your big-picture work versus every little project.

The goal is not to fill up your profile with lots of work projects and experience. The goal is to highlight work experience that tells the story of how you got to where you are today. No one is going to review everything you've done in your career. Showcase your most important and relevant work.

If you have relevant part-time work projects, consulting engagements, side businesses, or speaking gigs, you could list these projects under a single "catch-all" position, or you might be able to add them to your "Projects" section and "Publications" section.

If your work history is straightforward, this section of your LinkedIn profile should be pretty simple to complete.

With each work experience entry, include the dates that you have served (or currently serve) in the position. When you enter the company name, you can link your position to the corresponding LinkedIn company page if one exists.

There is room for a lengthy description of up to one thousand characters (half of the space of your LinkedIn summary) of your work experience within each position. Again, be precise with these descriptions. Highlight expertise you gained that is relevant to the work you are doing currently.

You can also add and showcase related rich media for each position you've held, such as videos and presentations.

Any recommendations you have collected for past or current positions can be showcased under the corresponding position.

List Your Educational Background to Expand Your Network

Listing your educational background on LinkedIn is important because it opens up a connection opportunity. You can conduct alumni searches for all of the schools you have attended and select which years you want to view. You can also filter alumni searches by location and job function. Once you select job function, you can see the specific companies where your alumni are working!

Within your alumni search results, LinkedIn will show you the connections you have in common with each individual. Typically, the more connections you have in common with someone, the easier it is to find ways to connect with them. You also have the ability to send a personalized invitation to connect because of your alumni relationship. Personalize your invitation by mentioning your common school and/or common connections.

Leveraging alumni search on LinkedIn is a great way to grow your network with highly relevant connections. By providing LinkedIn with your education history, you open a door to finding these new connections.

If you have any educational experience where you spent time learning but did not receive an actual degree, you might consider including it in your profile. Why? This will open up more potential connections for you on LinkedIn.

I attended graduate school for three years, working toward an MBA. I didn't finish, but I did earn a certification that was relevant to my career in the process. Regardless, I list this educational experience in my LinkedIn profile. Instead of adding a degree, I added the phrase "Graduate Studies." By listing this educational experience, I have the ability to connect with the alumni from my graduate school!

Collect and Showcase Your Endorsements

Collecting and showcasing endorsements for the skills you have on your LinkedIn profile may not seem like a big deal, but LinkedIn endorsements are actually an important tool. Many members brush off endorsements as being worthless. They are far from it.

You can choose up to fifty skills to be endorsed for, and your 1st-degree connections can endorse you for any or all of these skills. You can also select and showcase your top ten skills on your profile. (When you edit your skills, you can actually move any of them up or down.)

For the top skills that you showcase, small avatars of those individuals who have endorsed you will show up next to each skill. Up to twelve endorsements will be displayed for each of your top ten skills. If all ten skills each have at least twelve endorsements, the "Endorsements" section of your profile will be completely populated. This is the ideal visual display of "social proof" you want to achieve for your profile in this section.

LinkedIn also shows an endorsement count for each skill you have listed, all the way up to ninety-nine endorsements. The goal is to earn ninety-nine plus endorsements for your top skills!

Social proof can be very powerful in establishing your credibility. Endorsements are a visual display of your competency in your top skills.

Make sure that you select skills to be endorsed that accurately reflect your experience and specialties. Choose skills that are representative of the language your ideal clients recognize and utilize. In other words, don't use fancy jargon. Get as specific as you can with the skills you list. There are plenty of general terms to choose from. The more specific you can be, the better. Ultimately, you will have to choose from skills that are predefined by LinkedIn.

The skills you select to be endorsed for are also incorporated into LinkedIn's search data. For example, one of my top skills is *social media marketing*. This means that I have the ability to show up in LinkedIn search results for this skill if it is relevant to the person who is conducting the search. LinkedIn search results are designed to be highly relevant and customized to the person searching based on profile data and network connections.

As a simple example, someone who lives in my city searching on LinkedIn for help with social media may see my profile in their search results. I might even show up closer to the top if we have multiple connections in common. This is how your skills and endorsements can impact your discoverability on LinkedIn.

The entire "Endorsements" section on your profile can also be moved up or down.

What is the best way to earn endorsements?

Simple. Endorse your 1st-degree connections liberally! It takes no time at all to go through and endorse a few of your connections daily. You could even ask your connections what skills they prefer to be endorsed for. This simple activity of endorsing your connections is meaningful. It can trigger the *Rule of Reciprocity* and many of your connections will endorse you in return.

Rather than giving blanket endorsements across numerous skills for a connection, be selective about it. Look for the skills they have that you know them to be most competent in.

If you are unable to display your endorsements on your profile due to company policy, you can hide them, but do not delete them! You can never get them back if you delete them, and you may want them back if you ever change jobs or careers.

When you receive endorsements from others, consider also sending them a thank-you message!

Make a Human Connection through Rich Media Content

The ability to add rich media content (video, audio podcasts, images, presentations, e-books) throughout your profile is something that makes LinkedIn quite unique. Rich media can bring your profile to life!

Integrating rich media into your profile is a great way to make a human connection and showcase your insights in a variety of formats. You can demonstrate your expertise more effectively!

You can include rich media content in your LinkedIn "Summary" and "Work Experience" sections of your profile. Although you can add multiple pieces of content in each space, showcase your best work. Most people are not going to take the time to go through all of the rich content you have posted.

Do you have video footage from a recent speaking engagement or interview? What about a slide presentation that tells your personal brand story or a video introducing yourself?

In order for your media to display properly, it needs to be compatible with LinkedIn's supported providers. If you want to add a video, for example, you will want to add it from YouTube or Vimeo. For slide presentations, you would add them from SlideShare. You can also add podcast episodes from SoundCloud.

If you enter your own web links here, the visual will not render properly on your profile and will not look as professional as media that is supported by LinkedIn. When adding your rich media, you will see a link to further explore LinkedIn's supported providers.

Visit profiles of individuals in your industry or people who influence you. What are they showcasing on LinkedIn? You may be able to get some ideas to build from.

Don't neglect this fantastic opportunity to make your profile more dynamic and memorable. Your rich media can be a significant differentiator. Your profile visitors can really see who you are and connect with you on a more personal level, especially with video and audio.

Think Outside the Box with "Projects" and "Publications"

"Projects" and "Publications" are the only sections of your profile where you can actually link to your content or third-party content. Not only can you utilize these sections to enhance your credibility, you can showcase and link to your own content here as well.

For your "Projects" section, share relevant work that would be important for a potential client to see. The "Projects" section is great for work you've done that doesn't fit under your current or past work experiences. For example, have you run workshops or webinars, or recorded speaking presentations that you can link to here? You can also add consulting work that you've done or any projects that deserve visibility.

Your "Publications" section is a great place to link to your blog, any guides or e-books you may offer, books you have authored, and third-party publications where you have contributed or been featured.

For both "Projects" and "Publications," you can include a title, description, date, and link. The title you enter will actually point to the web link you insert.

In the "Publications" section, I list a complimentary e-book that links directly to a landing page on my website where someone can opt-in and receive the guide instantly.

Taking advantage of the "Projects" and "Publications" sections will allow you to expand on your expertise and strategically drive traffic to your own educational offers on your website.

Add Your Volunteer Work, Awards and Certifications, Associations, and Causes

In keeping with the goal of completing your LinkedIn profile, do your best to complete every section I've listed above. When you do, you create more and more connection points and you make LinkedIn smarter about you.

Adding volunteer experience can be a valuable way to make connections with others in your community. Awards and certifications enhance your professional credibility. Listing the associations you are a member of can show your commitment to your work, industry, or profession.

Don't forget to include your date of birth. When you do, your network will be notified about your birthday and be prompted to send you a message. When your connections have birthdays, take the time to send each of them a personalized message! This is a subtle way to acknowledge the people in your network once a year on their special day!

Include Contact Information in Your Profile

In the "Advice for Contacting You" section of your profile, it's important to add descriptive contact information to make it easier for your profile viewers to reach out to you. This section of your profile is open-ended, which means it's a blank canvas to enter whatever you deem appropriate for your business.

In this section of my profile, I point to my website and my primary call to action, which is a free guide. I also link to my Twitter account and Facebook page here and encourage viewers to connect with me on those channels as well. Because it is a blank canvas, you can explain how you *prefer* to be contacted.

Depending on your business model, you may want to include your phone number and e-mail address. Just be aware that when you list your e-mail, people who don't know you can send you an invitation to connect if they find this in your "Contact Information" section. Your e-mail may also be susceptible to being scraped by certain software programs. I've had to remove my e-mail address from this section of my profile for these reasons.

On the flip side, if you are looking to connect with someone and don't have any way to do so without their e-mail address, check this section of their LinkedIn profile. Many times the e-mail address will be listed here.

Add Your Interests and Leverage for Connection

Adding interests to your profile is not only simple, it's another valuable way to get discovered via LinkedIn search. It's also a way for your connections to learn more about you. When you add your interests, include both professional and personal interests. Separate each of your interests with a comma.

Interests are discoverable within LinkedIn search. This means someone can find you based on your interests, or you can find people to connect with based on their interests. You can also search your 1st-, 2nd-, Group-, and 3rd-level connections for specific interests.

I did an advanced LinkedIn search of my 1st-degree connections for the keyword "snowboarding." My search results showed thirty-four of my 1st-degree connections also had snowboarding listed as an interest. These are thirty-four people I'm already connected to. Now I can engage with each of these individuals around a common interest! It gives me a great excuse to connect and strike up a conversation.

You can also find groups to join based on your interests. I ran the same "snowboarding" search but this time allowed LinkedIn to find all results for me, not just my 1st-degree connections. The results showed over ninety LinkedIn groups for "snowboarding."

Joining groups based on common interests that members are passionate about is a great way to discover, engage, and connect with new people.

Lastly, review the interests of your clients, prospects, and important connections. This information can come in handy when you engage with people who are important to your business!

Connect Your LinkedIn Profile to Your Twitter Account

In the settings area of your LinkedIn account, you can add your Twitter account. When you do this, your Twitter handle will be displayed under the "Contact Info" tab near the top of your profile. Viewers of your profile can click the link to go and connect with you on Twitter. The other benefit of adding your Twitter account to your profile is that you can share LinkedIn status updates simultaneously to your Twitter account.

When you share a status update, if you select the *Share with: Public + Twitter* option, your update will also be shared to Twitter.

Set Your Profile Up for Maximum Visibility

The number one rule for being visible on LinkedIn is to **complete your profile**. Don't leave any part of your profile blank! You are not finished building your LinkedIn profile until you reach "All-Star" status. (LinkedIn will give you your status in the sidebar of your profile.) Don't stop until you become an All-Star!

There are a number of account settings that pertain to your profile on LinkedIn that you will want to review to make sure you are completely visible to the maximum number of people. Whenever I review LinkedIn profiles for my clients, I almost always see that their settings are not configured for maximum visibility.

Visit your LinkedIn "Privacy & Settings" to adjust these settings.

In order to maximize your profile visibility, there are a few settings to double check.

Under the "Profile" tab in your "Privacy & Settings," you will see an option to *change your profile photo visibility*. This link will take you to your LinkedIn photo where you can select who can see the image. I recommend setting this to "Everyone," making your headshot visible beyond your connections and network.

Also under the "Profile" tab in "Privacy & Settings," select "Everyone" for *who can see your activity feed* and *choose who can follow your updates*. If you limit the visibility of your activity and updates to just your connections, you limit your reach on LinkedIn.

There is one more section to check to make sure your profile is visible. In your top navigation menu, select the option to "Edit Profile." Next to the blue button that says "View Profile As," there is an arrow that will show a dropdown menu when you hover over it. There you will see an option to "Manage public profile settings." This will take you to a view of your public profile. There you can select which sections of your profile you would like to be visible. I make ALL sections of my profile visible.

There are a couple of settings you will want to think about, such as deciding who can see your connections and whether or not to show *your* profile details when viewing other profiles. If possible, I recommend allowing your connections to be visible (unless you don't want competitors to see) and keeping your profile visible when you view other people's profiles.

Limiting who can see your connections will limit your network growth. Making your profile visible when viewing other profiles will generate interest. Many people will view you back and invite you to connect!

Lastly, I do suggest turning OFF your activity broadcasts in your settings. This option will hide when you update your profile, make recommendations, or follow companies. You don't want to broadcast when you make changes to your profile, especially if you tweak it frequently like I do!

Profile Discovery in LinkedIn Search

You can be discovered within LinkedIn's own *internal* people-search engine based on how you build out your profile. Your profile will also most likely rank in the top five Google search results for your name (unless you have a very common name).

LinkedIn's internal search has continued to become more and more powerful. When search numbers were last reported by LinkedIn back in 2012, there were nearly **six billion people searches** that year. That number has continued to grow.

The reason LinkedIn's search engine is so powerful is the relevancy of the results. LinkedIn dramatically improved its search algorithm in January 2015 for relevancy and personalization. They also expanded search results for members with free accounts to see 1st-, 2nd-, and 3rd-degree connections (previously, this was limited).

LinkedIn now incorporates shared or common connections, groups, and companies into its search results. This means you can see overlap in these areas when conducting people searches on LinkedIn.

Your profile data is also integrated into LinkedIn search results. Posts that you publish on the LinkedIn Publishing Platform or SlideShare content you upload can also be found in LinkedIn search results if relevant to particular keywords.

The smarter you make LinkedIn about you through your profile, your connections, and the content you upload or post to the platform, the greater the opportunity to be found by the right people. I'll discuss how to effectively use LinkedIn search in greater detail later in the book.

Promote Your LinkedIn Profile

To continue growing your network with relevant connections, there are numerous ways to promote your LinkedIn profile outside of LinkedIn.

Add your LinkedIn profile URL to your e-mail signature and business card. Link to your profile from your website. Whenever you do a speaking engagement or podcast interview, invite attendees and listeners to connect with you on LinkedIn. I usually ask people to mention where they saw or heard me so I will know to accept the invitation to connect!

You can also create an embeddable profile snippet for your website with <u>this tool here</u>.

Promote your LinkedIn profile across other social media channels like Facebook and Twitter. An easy way to do this is to ask this question in your status update: "Are we connected on LinkedIn yet? Send me an invite!"

Why You Need a LinkedIn Company Page

Even if you are a solo entrepreneur, a LinkedIn company page is a good idea for your business for a number of reasons.

First, when you create a company page, you create another positive digital asset for your business that can be found in search engines like Google and Bing.

Next, you can build followers for your company page and share status updates with your followers, just like you can with your personal profile. However, I have found that company page status updates get more visibility and engagement than the updates you post to your personal profile!

Another huge benefit to a LinkedIn company page is the ability to run direct sponsored updates (ads) on LinkedIn. Direct sponsored updates look like normal LinkedIn status updates. They are native to the LinkedIn news feed. The only difference is your sponsored updates will be identified as "sponsored."

As organic visibility and engagement continues to decline across most of the major social media platforms, the next wave is paid social ads. LinkedIn ads are not nearly as saturated yet as ads on other social platforms. The ability to target professionals through LinkedIn ads is also unmatched. You can't find the same kind of targeting capabilities anywhere on the Internet.

Creating a LinkedIn company page is easy. Enter your basic company information, as well as a description and a link to your website. You can also upload a graphic header for your company page.

SlideShare

LinkedIn owns SlideShare. SlideShare in and of itself is a very powerful content channel for growing your visibility and influence. SlideShare continues to exist as a separate site from LinkedIn, but the two are integrated very tightly.

You will need to create a SlideShare profile and give LinkedIn permission to access it (you will see this option within your SlideShare settings). As I mentioned previously, you can link to your SlideShare content in the "Summary" and "Work Experience" sections of your LinkedIn profile.

When you share content from SlideShare as a status update on LinkedIn, viewers of your update can view the presentation without ever leaving LinkedIn.

With SlideShare, you are not limited to slide presentations. You can also upload PDF and video content to your profile.

One killer feature of SlideShare is the ability to collect leads from the viewers of your content. This works especially well if you have a presentation in SlideShare that gets significant visibility. I've been able to generate a significant number of qualified leads through a single SlideShare presentation that received more than six thousand views. This is now a paid SlideShare feature. Expect to pay dollars for leads and make sure the cost per lead fits with your business model.

SlideShare is a great opportunity for demonstrating your knowledge and expertise more visually. This powerful, visual content channel is becoming more popular. Consider turning some of your blog posts into presentations. You can also upload PDF files such as guides and e-books, as well as incorporate videos into SlideShare.

Now is the perfect time to start leveraging SlideShare in conjunction with LinkedIn to grow your influence.

As you can see, there is a lot of work that goes into powering up your LinkedIn profile with *precision*. This is a strategic and ongoing process. You really need to think through exactly who it is that you want to reach on LinkedIn.

If you are diligent about completing and optimizing your profile for that specific ideal client, it will become a magnet for your business. Your LinkedIn profile truly is the gateway to attracting your ideal clients, building a powerful referral network, driving quality website traffic, and growing your personal influence.

Now, let's move on to the next rule and talk about why and how to build a smarter LinkedIn network!

Chapter 2

RULE #2—Build a Smarter Network

> *Your network is your net worth.*
>
> - John Maxwell

Have you ever wondered which LinkedIn invitations to accept or decline? Most LinkedIn members struggle with this.

Your LinkedIn network is one of the most valuable professional assets you can build today. Your LinkedIn network can lead to relationships and opportunities you may have never thought possible. However, if your network consists of random connections, you will probably make things a lot tougher on yourself.

When you focus on building a *smarter network* on LinkedIn, the professional relationships and business opportunities you attract will be much more meaningful and relevant.

Just as I've suggested you use precision when building your LinkedIn profile, I want you to think the same way about your network. A smarter LinkedIn network makes LinkedIn smarter about you.

Wouldn't you prefer to have your profile viewed by the people you actually want to connect with or work with? Wouldn't you prefer that LinkedIn show you *relevant* professionals you should be connecting with? Wouldn't you like to show up in the results of searches conducted by your ideal clients and referral sources?

Building a *smarter network* on LinkedIn creates a more linear path to business success. Simply put, a smarter network allows you to have an impact and build your personal influence with the *right* people.

The Three Advantages of a Smarter LinkedIn Network

When you focus on connecting with the right people on LinkedIn, you increase the probability of attracting the right opportunities to your business. Additionally, if you know whom you are connected with on LinkedIn, you will better understand what they value and know what to share.

An intelligent network on LinkedIn can be a gold mine. A random network, no matter how big or small, will dilute your success.

Here are the three main advantages of building a smart LinkedIn network:

- **Advantage #1:** Once you connect with someone and accept them into your LinkedIn network, you have the opportunity to stay *consistently* visible and valuable to them. Out of network = out of sight = out of mind. In network = interest.
- **Advantage #2:** When you make a new connection on LinkedIn, you gain the *privilege* of going one-to-one with that person through LinkedIn messaging. That means you can start private conversations with important people.
- **Advantage #3:** Making smarter connections on LinkedIn will give you exposure to more relevant connections at the 2nd- and 3rd-degree network levels. The strategy automatically builds upon itself.

Building a smarter network on LinkedIn will cut your workload in half when it comes to finding and attracting business opportunities. Your network will end up doing the work for you.

The LinkedIn Network Effect

One of the most powerful aspects of LinkedIn is the network effect. Your LinkedIn network stretches far beyond your 1st-degree connections. Even though your 1st-degree connections are going to see more of your LinkedIn activities, you have the potential to reach your 2nd- and 3rd-degree connections.

If a 1st-degree connection engages with one of your status updates, for example, their connections (your 2nd-degree network) have the potential to see the update and conversation. Let's take it a step further. If one of your 2nd-degree connections engages with your post, their connections have the potential to see the conversation (your 3rd-degree connections).

It is literally possible for something you post on LinkedIn to gain visibility with your 3rd-degree network. This is the power of the *LinkedIn network effect*. Your reach can be expanded by three degrees! If you have one hundred connections and I have one hundred connections, between us we have ten thousand potential connections, not just two hundred.

We don't discover people randomly on social networks. Most often, we discover interesting new people to connect with through our existing network. Think about people you have been exposed to online who have influenced you. You can most likely trace that discovery back to someone within your existing network. This is due to the power of social sharing and the fact that we trust what the members of our networks endorse!

I have found a life-changing business coach, website designer, lawyer, and bookkeeper all through my LinkedIn network. The same can happen for you as members of your network share or promote your work with their connections. This is why it is so important to create meaningful and relevant content on a consistent basis.

The smarter and more relevant your LinkedIn network, the more powerful the *LinkedIn network effect*.

Who You Know Still Matters

According to Nielsen, 92 percent of people trust recommendations from friends and family.

I touched on the power and ease of social network referrals in a previous chapter (Rule #1). If you want to earn referrals from your existing clients, customers, partners, and advocates of your business, get connected with these individuals on LinkedIn. Replicate your offline network, online.

Start with the network you already have and build on that foundation with LinkedIn. By connecting with your important existing contacts, you will also be able to consistently reinforce those relationships in new ways.

Your existing contacts can play a significant role in growing your personal influence on LinkedIn. They will be some of your biggest advocates. They will engage with you. They will promote your content. They will lead you to people who are just like them, and they will refer your clients.

Build a "Right-Sized" LinkedIn Network

More connections on LinkedIn will not equal greater success. At one point in my LinkedIn journey, I believed just the opposite of this and ended up learning the hard way. Because of that false belief, I still have to prune my network constantly to clean it up and improve the quality.

Rob Cross is a University of Virginia professor for the McIntire School of Commerce.[1] Through his research, Cross has studied networks of high performers across a wide range of organizations and found that having a large network was not a reason for success. Cross concluded, "There is a negative

---

[1] Rob Cross is a University of Virginia Professor in the McIntire School of Commerce. The research referenced in this passage is derived from a Harvard Business Review article co-authored by Rob Cross entitled "A Smarter Way to Network."

statistically significant likelihood of being a top performer and knowing a lot of people."

The quantity of LinkedIn connections you have is only as valuable as the relevancy and depth of each of those connections. When you grow your network with *relevant* connections and go deeper with the important few, you attract more of the same.

As a reference point, most LinkedIn users have between 500–999 connections and less than 20 percent of users have more than one thousand connections.[2] LinkedIn stops showing how many connections you have beyond five hundred. I do think it is important to get to the five hundred mark (as long as you are making quality connections). That number does carry some social proof with your LinkedIn presence.

The Power of an Open Network

Ron Burt, a leading network scientist from the University of Chicago, studies how our networks affect our careers and businesses. His groundbreaking research revealed that people who have an **open network** are significantly more successful than those who have a closed network, and being in an open network is an extremely strong predictor of business or career success.[3]

According to Burt's network science work, we don't just have one giant network. Instead, we develop *network clusters*. A network cluster represents a group of connections who share something in common, such as location, industry, school, values, beliefs, interests, and other psychographic qualities.

An **open network** consists of *multiple* network clusters. The ability to cross connect between network clusters is what leads to greater networking success. When we build and participate in an

---

[2] Source: Power+Formula 2014 LinkedIn User Survey by Wayne Breitbarth.

[3] Ron Burt is a University of Chicago Professor and leading academic researcher on how social networks create career and business advantages.
http://www.chicagobooth.edu/faculty/directory/b/ronald-s-burt

open network, we gain exposure to new ideas, people, and economic opportunities.

Having a single network cluster would represent a *closed network*. Within a closed network, we tend to fall into groupthink. Closed networks reaffirm what we already believe. The same ideas are constantly regurgitated.

Burt's research concluded that being a part of an **open network** is an extremely strong predictor of career (or business) success. High performers tend to have open networks.

When you think about growing a strategic LinkedIn network, think about connecting with people across the multiple network clusters you belong to. These clusters also represent your *unique market opportunities*, which I will cover in more detail later in this chapter.

Some examples of closed networks include millennials and baby boomers, or Democrats and Republicans. Imagine cross connecting people and ideas between these network clusters. It would probably be challenging. Burt's research showed significant promise for people who have the ability to "broker" ideas and relationships *between* their network clusters.

I personally have two prominent industry network clusters, financial services and digital business and marketing. The conversations, ideas, and experiences differ within each of these clusters. However, I'm able to take a concept from one network and make it applicable to the other. For example, I can teach financial advisors the digital marketing strategies that I know would work well for them because I understand their business model.

When you start viewing your LinkedIn network as an open network with multiple clusters, it will open up new opportunities for cross connecting people and ideas. Being an open networker can also help you grow your influence within each of the network clusters you belong to. Being an open networker is a competitive advantage.

Understanding and Leveraging LinkedIn's Social Graph

LinkedIn has redefined the six degrees of separation through its professional social graph, and it just keeps getting better.

Because of all of the member data LinkedIn has collected from its almost four hundred million members, they are able to map out who we are connected to and how we are connected.

For example, LinkedIn knows our common connections with others, our common educational and work experience, common locations, members we are similar to, members we share skills and expertise with, members we share interests with, members we share groups with, and more.

This "people intelligence" is incredibly valuable, and as a LinkedIn member, you get access to much of this data! (Premium LinkedIn members get more access.)

When you view profiles of your 1st-degree connections, 2nd-degree connections, and mutual group members, you can see the following information (profiles of 3rd-degree connections you don't share any groups with are only visible with certain premium-level accounts):

- How you are connected (connections in common)
- Common groups, education, location, skills, and expertise
- People also viewed (other profiles that were viewed)
- People similar to the person you are viewing

LinkedIn is leaving you a trail of breadcrumbs to help you discover relevant people to connect with. Pay attention to these clues!

When you can see the shared connections and professional points of overlap with the members in your extended LinkedIn network, you can leverage this information to expand your 1st-degree network more intelligently.

LinkedIn is constantly helping you build a smarter network. Your job is to pay attention to the data and do your research!

LinkedIn "New Connection" Etiquette

My number one rule of thumb for making new connections on LinkedIn is to send **personalized invitations** whenever possible. Unfortunately, this is getting tougher to do. Even when you have the best of intentions, you may end up sending a generic invitation.

Sending personalized invitations to the people you want to connect with gives you a few major advantages. Your personalized invitations will stand out, build rapport, and achieve higher acceptance rates.

If you want to connect with someone on LinkedIn but do not meet LinkedIn's requirements to send a personalized invitation (colleague, classmate, have done business together, friend), you will need to have an e-mail address for the person you wish to connect with. I'll talk more about how to connect with people you don't know later in this chapter.

Be aware that there are numerous instances where you can click a "connect" button on LinkedIn and unintentionally bypass the personalized invitation screen. This will result in sending a generic invitation. When you don't meet any of LinkedIn's requirements for sending personalized invitations, either you won't be able to send an invitation at all or you will send a generic invitation when you click that "connect" button.

The one positive of a generic invitation, if there is one, is that the recipient will still be able to see your picture and your LinkedIn headline summary. If your headline summary is highly relevant, they will likely view your profile. If your profile is impressive, they will likely accept your generic invitation.

If you do send a generic invitation and it is accepted, quickly send a follow-up thank-you message and explain why you sent the invitation. Also, explain that you were not able to customize the invitation. This usually works very well!

Another strategy is to consider sending an introductory InMail message first if you are unable to send a personalized invitation to someone you wish to connect with. InMails are paid messages that can be sent to anyone on LinkedIn. They are accessible through premium LinkedIn accounts. I'll talk more about how to utilize InMails later in the chapter.

Premium account members on LinkedIn can choose to indicate that they have an "open profile." If you have the open profile feature enabled, anyone can send you a message and view your profile, even if they are not part of your 1st-degree network. You would have the same access to anyone on LinkedIn with an open profile whether you have a premium or free LinkedIn account.

Having an open profile will give you more visibility on LinkedIn. Just be aware that you eventually may start receiving messages from people you don't know, some of which will be solicitations.

Send Personalized Thank-Yous to New Connections

The best time to build rapport with someone is right after you have connected with them on LinkedIn. Sending a personalized thank-you message is the perfect way to do this. It's also a great way for a new connection to learn more about you.

To save time, you can create a thank-you script to copy and paste into your messages. You can customize around your scripted message, which I do recommend.

In your message, thank the person for connecting with you. Consider asking questions that build rapport such as, "What type of clients do you work with?" This is a great way to determine who you can introduce them to from your network.

Create an e-mail signature for your thank-you message that includes a link to your website. I've seen excellent response rates with these thank-you messages!

Thank-you messages are an effective way to stand out and become more memorable to the new connections you make on LinkedIn.

Import Your Existing Contacts into LinkedIn (and Make LinkedIn Smarter About You)

I have a Nest thermostat in my home. When it was first installed, it worked like any other thermostat because it didn't understand my preferences and behaviors. There was nothing smart about it.

After the first few weeks, my Nest thermostat became brilliant! It knew when to turn the heat or air on and off at my preferred times and temperatures.

LinkedIn works in this way when it comes to collecting data about us. The more data you provide to LinkedIn about who you are, who your contacts are, and what you care about, the more relevant and meaningful your experience is going to be.

A great way to jump-start your smart network building is to import your existing contacts into LinkedIn (don't worry, you can export your data at any time). The easiest way to do this is to connect your e-mail account with LinkedIn.

When you do this, LinkedIn will go through your contact list and show you whether or not you are connected with each contact on LinkedIn. You will make LinkedIn smarter about your existing network. This was something I talked about earlier in this chapter. Your existing contacts matter.

LinkedIn will also sync your contacts on an ongoing basis after the initial import as long as you connect your primary e-mail provider. This comes in handy for new contacts you collect outside of LinkedIn.

(Keep in mind that LinkedIn will also have access to your e-mail communications and your calendar if you choose these options.)

Once you sync your existing contacts with LinkedIn, you will be able to go through them one-by-one and send personalized invitations to anyone you are not already connected to.

Although this can be time consuming if you have a sizable e-mail list, it is very worthwhile. I suggest going through a few contacts each day until you get through the list.

Warning! Make sure not to send a generic invitation to all of these contacts at one time. Skip this option if it is offered by LinkedIn. It does not work well, especially if any of your contacts are unfamiliar with LinkedIn.

I also recommend cleaning up your e-mail list before you upload it to LinkedIn. It will save you time as you sort through your contacts and send invitations to connect on LinkedIn.

Leverage Your Unique Market Opportunities

The best way to determine whether or not to connect with someone on LinkedIn beyond your existing contacts is to understand your *unique market opportunities*.

Your *unique market opportunities* include people who fall into the following categories:

- location (where you live and work)
- industry (past and present)
- referral sources
- natural affinity markets (shared qualities or characteristics)
- friends of friends (or connections of your connections)
- relevant influencers
- hobbies/interests
- associations or organizations you belong to
- conference or event attendees
- community or charitable causes

There should be a good reason for why you would accept or send an invitation to connect with anyone on LinkedIn. Don't evaluate making a connection based on whether or not you personally know someone; evaluate making a connection based on your *unique market opportunities*. Does the potential connection fit with one of your criteria?

LinkedIn discourages connecting with people you don't know. However, there are many ways to identify common connection points to leverage with almost any LinkedIn member you want to reach. If you can establish a base level of rapport with someone founded on a shared interest, industry, group, or connection, it would not be out of the ordinary to send an invitation to connect.

I recommend connecting with influencers, journalists, and editors in your community and/or industry (94 percent of editors and journalists are on LinkedIn[4]), even if you don't know them personally.

Most of these professionals are well connected and active on LinkedIn. Don't look for media professionals and influencers to help you out. Instead, look for ways to serve as a resource and give value. Build relationships with these important people.

Also, I recommend connecting with people who resonate with you based on your perspective, values, and beliefs. For example, I will accept LinkedIn invitations from people who mention that they have heard me speak. These individuals can become your biggest advocates!

Map out your own *unique market opportunities* to build a smarter network on LinkedIn. Once you know exactly with whom you want to connect, you can accelerate the network-building process.

Find the "Low-Hanging Fruit" Connections

There are some obvious LinkedIn connections to make that result from going about your daily work and social life that you may not be thinking about. If you start to become more aware of formalizing these connections on LinkedIn, you can steadily grow your network with very qualified people.

---

[4] A media survey by Arketi Media Group revealed that over 94% of journalists and editors are on LinkedIn, and 62% rate it as their preferred professional networking tool.

Here are some examples of "low-hanging fruit" connections:

1) Top-of-Mind Connections

Top-of-mind connections are the people you meet in person, or have phone calls or e-mail exchanges with. These are also the people you come into contact with in the course of your daily work, family, and social life.

For example, another parent sitting in the bleachers at your kid's basketball or soccer game might be someone you would want to connect with on LinkedIn. Another example is the owner of a local business or restaurant where you are a frequent patron.

Top-of-mind connections can include people you've interacted with for the first time or people you already know but haven't connected with on LinkedIn.

2) Alumni

I have found LinkedIn's alumni search tool to be one of the most effective ways to find relevant connections. You can filter alumni people searches on LinkedIn by where they live, where they work, what they do, what they are skilled at, and how you are connected with them (1st-, 2nd-, 3rd-degree or group members).

It doesn't matter how many people you knew when you went to school. Sharing a common school or university is a very powerful way to get your foot in the door with new connections.

3) Cross Connect on Other Social Networks

If you are on LinkedIn, you are likely also on Facebook and Twitter. You may engage with people on these networks that you have not connected with officially on LinkedIn. This can also work the other way around. Export your LinkedIn connections and find those who are also on Twitter and Facebook! (Note: you will need to first export your LinkedIn connections into an e-mail service like Gmail before you can import into Twitter or Facebook.)

4) People You May Know

The "People You May Know" feature is where LinkedIn suggests people for you to connect with. In some cases, these suggestions don't make sense, but as LinkedIn becomes smarter about you and your network, they will become more relevant.

5) Rekindle Dormant Ties

Dormant ties are those where you may have had a relationship or acquaintance at some point in time but you are not connected on LinkedIn. Dormant ties can include people you have known from prior jobs, places you have lived, and schools you have attended, to name a few. Adam Grant, author of the New York Times bestselling *Give and Take*, suggests that dormant ties can lead to strong ties because you have a history and shared experience. This makes it quicker and more comfortable to reconnect.

The Value of Your 2nd-Degree Connections

If you are doing your diligence to build a smart 1st-degree network on LinkedIn, your 2nd-degree connections are going to be that much more relevant. These are the people who are connected with your 1st-degree connections.

You are only one degree away from your 2nd-degree connections on LinkedIn, and you can actually see who these individuals are!

The best way to identify your 2nd-degree connections is by using LinkedIn's advanced search tool. Select the 2nd-degree filter for your search and narrow the search by geographical location, industry, job title, or any other parameter available to you.

You can also directly search the connections of your 1st-degree network, as long as they have made their connections public. Identify and search the connections of your *best* clients and professional partners. Who are the people in their networks that you want to know?

Search the network of a 1st-degree connection directly from his or her profile. Use the small search box above their list of connections and narrow your search by adding a location, industry, or specific keyword into the box.

Groups are another place to surface relevant 2nd-degree connections. Visit the groups you belong to and search the list of mutual group members. Again, narrow your searches with various parameters and/or keywords to make them more relevant.

When attempting to connect with a 2nd-degree connection, I recommend first sending a message to your mutual 1st-degree connection. Explain who you would like to connect with and give your reason. Ask for permission to use their name in the process.

Taking the initiative to make an introduction rather than asking your contact to do this work for you is much more effective. Be careful about using LinkedIn's introduction tool. The tool is a bit confusing to most LinkedIn members who are not familiar with it. More important, your contact will have to do the work of making the introduction.

When you initiate the introduction process and take control of it, your 1st-degree connection will not be required to do all the work for you! Keep in mind that not everyone knows each of his or her 1st-degree connections personally. You might ask "How well do you know [insert name]?" in your message to begin with.

When possible, send a personalized invitation to your 2nd-degree connections. You may need to send an InMail message first to establish rapport prior to sending an invitation to connect.

Pay Attention to Shared Connections

LinkedIn will show you the connections you have in common with your 2nd- and 3rd-degree connections, as well as mutual group members.

This feature alone is one of the most powerful benefits of building your online network on LinkedIn. You have this unique ability to peek into your extended network.

When you can see the connections you have in common with thousands of LinkedIn members, you can determine who might be a good fit for your smart network.

LinkedIn shows your shared connections with other members in multiple places such as member profiles, the alumni area, the "Who's Viewed Your Profile," and the "People You May Know" sections. Just look for the icon of overlapping circles and hover over it to see the list of connections you share with another LinkedIn member.

There is a direct correlation between the number of shared connections you have with someone on LinkedIn and the likelihood they will accept your invitation to connect.

When I come across someone I would like to connect with on LinkedIn and see that we have numerous shared connections, I will mention this in my personalized invitation or InMail in order to establish rapport.

Typically, I send a message or invitation that says:

"Hello [Insert Name], I came across your profile recently and it looks like we know a lot of the same people! I thought it would make sense for us to also connect here on LinkedIn."

Review the common connections you share with your 1st-degree network. Are there ways you can bring groups of these professionals together for a lunch or dinner meeting? This is one of many ideas for leveraging the connections you have in common with others in your network.

Note that LinkedIn members can adjust their privacy settings to hide who their connections are. You can do the same, but I don't recommend this. Instead, you might select the option to only allow *your connections* to see whom you are connected to. That way, if you are worried about your competitors seeing your connections, you can just not connect with your competitors!

When you better understand how you are connected to others on LinkedIn, you can use that data to your advantage in building a smarter and more in-depth network.

Connecting with People You Don't Know

By now you know how important it is to build your network with the people you do know, such as your existing contacts. However, LinkedIn is a very powerful tool for connecting with important people you don't know (or don't know well).

When you connect with people you don't know but should know, you can open all kinds of doors to new opportunities. My business would not be where it is today if I had decided to only connect with the people I know well.

The prerequisite for connecting with LinkedIn members you don't know is to make sure they fit your *unique market opportunities* criteria (discussed earlier in the chapter).

When sending an invite to someone you don't know (or don't know well), I highly recommend sending a personalized invitation. If you don't meet LinkedIn's rules for sending a personalized invitation, try to locate the person's e-mail address. Check their LinkedIn profile or look elsewhere online. If you have an e-mail address for the person, you can send a personalized invitation using the "other" option that LinkedIn provides.

If you are unable to locate an e-mail address, I recommend sending an InMail message. Set the stage with this message for sending a follow-up invitation to connect. InMails are messages you can send to anyone on LinkedIn, whether you are connected or not. They are only available with premium LinkedIn accounts. I'll cover these in more depth later in the book.

The one downside to sending an InMail is that you have to choose from a menu of predefined reasons that describe why you are sending the message. These predefined reasons don't always fit. However, you can make up for this with a compelling subject line that grabs attention.

For all InMails you send that are responded to, LinkedIn will credit you back the InMail. With an InMail, you have significant space to send a lengthy message. I suggest keeping your message short and to the point. Make sure to mention in your InMail message that you are going to also send an invitation to connect.

I have found this process to work very well for connecting with people I don't know on LinkedIn. Within my InMail messages, I almost always reference a common professional point or connection in order to build some rapport.

View Profiles of the People You Wish to Connect With

Did you realize that "Who's Viewed Your Profile" is one of the most popular features on LinkedIn? LinkedIn members love the ability to see who is looking at them!

A little-known tactic for attracting new, strategic connections on LinkedIn is to go out and view the profiles of the people you are interested in connecting with. Make sure your profile settings are configured to show your identity when viewing the profiles of other members.

When you view someone's profile, they can see your profile image and headline summary, as well as the connections you have in common.

When you view profiles of the people you would like to connect with, many of them will view you back. A percentage of those individuals will then send you an invitation to connect or even a message leading with, "I saw that you viewed my profile…"

Viewing profiles of those professionals you want to connect with creates a subtle, warm connection with them. It is human nature to want to "view back" the profiles of people who are looking at you.

Check out those who have viewed your profile on a daily basis if you can. View their profiles, and if it makes sense to connect or send a message, do so!

You may also find some of your 1st-degree connections are viewing your profile as well. This can be a result of increasing your LinkedIn activity level. When you see current connections who have viewed your profile, this is a good time to touch base and check in with a personalized message.

Recently, a handful of software tools have come out claiming to automate your profile viewing activity on LinkedIn. Be very careful if you use any of these tools as they could potentially cause your LinkedIn account to be flagged or shut down!

Use LinkedIn Groups to Make Relevant Connections

While many LinkedIn groups are full of self-serving promotional posts, why not use them instead to build your network? There are millions of LinkedIn members who belong to groups, yet they are no longer active in these groups for a variety of reasons.

As I mentioned previously, you can search through the membership of a group that you belong to from the main group page. Simply click on the "Members" tab to access the search box.

Mine your LinkedIn group memberships and utilize groups for relevant professionals you can connect with who fit into your smart network-building strategy.

One special benefit you get by joining relevant LinkedIn groups is the ability to send private, personalized messages to mutual group members. Note that you are limited to fifteen total messages per month to mutual group members, so use them wisely.

To run advanced LinkedIn searches across ALL of the groups that you belong to at one time, you will need a premium account.

Don't overlook LinkedIn groups as an opportunity for finding relevant connections to build your smart network.

Find Potential Connections with LinkedIn's Advanced Search

With LinkedIn's recent revamping of its search engine for speed and relevance, there is no better way to find the right professionals to connect with.

One of the primary ways that LinkedIn is making its internal search engine better is by showing you results based on your existing network connections.

If you are building a smart network as I'm teaching you to do in this chapter, your LinkedIn search results should be highly relevant. You also have the opportunity to show up in any LinkedIn member's searches that are relevant to you and your network.

Premium accounts get more search filters and the ability to save searches. With a saved search, each time a LinkedIn member meets your search criteria, they will be added to your search results list. There are a good number of search filters you get access to as a free LinkedIn member as well.

Let me share an example with you to demonstrate the power of LinkedIn's advanced search. I was interested in putting together a small group mastermind dinner with ten to fifteen female entrepreneurs in my city. I conducted an advanced search with filters for a specific national women's LinkedIn group I belong to, my local zip code, 1st- and 2nd-degree connections only, and the keywords "CEO" or "Owner" or "President."

My search returned thirty-three results. From those results, I identified the twenty women I felt would be the best fit for my event and sent each of them a personalized message. I sent my 2nd-degree connections in this group InMail messages followed by invitations to connect.

There are limitless combinations you can utilize for finding exactly the people you want to connect with on LinkedIn through the advanced search tool. I do recommend becoming more familiar with Boolean search operators in order to get the most accurate results possible.

With Boolean search, you can use search operators such as AND, OR, NOT, and () in your searches. Do a quick Google search for "LinkedIn Boolean cheat sheet" and you will find a downloadable PDF from LinkedIn. Learning and leveraging these Boolean search operators can help you target your searches more effectively.

Connect through Other Social Networks First

A great way to get on the radar of someone you would like to connect with on LinkedIn is to *first* engage on other social networks. Twitter is my favorite, because there are no limitations on who you can follow or @mention publicly. (You might also be able to send a direct message on Twitter.)

When you utilize a social network like Twitter to build rapport with someone first, they will be much more likely to recognize and accept your invitation to connect on LinkedIn.

A marketing professional approached me exactly in this way. First, he shared a public tweet promoting an article I had written and @mentioned me in the tweet. I thanked him on Twitter publicly for sharing my article. The next day I received a private message from him on LinkedIn with the subject line "From Twitter to LinkedIn." His message simply stated that he would love to connect on LinkedIn as well. I responded and provided him with my e-mail address so that he could send me an invitation.

It is likely that I would have never been receptive to an invitation to connect on LinkedIn from this person if I hadn't noticed him on Twitter first. The only reason I noticed him was because he promoted my content to his followers!

This can work for you as well. If there is someone you would like to connect with on LinkedIn, promote their work on another social network first!

Make New Connections through Companies

Over three million companies have pages on LinkedIn. Chances are many companies in your city or town have a company page.

Have you ever thought about mining those LinkedIn company pages to find new connections? Start following relevant company pages to keep up with the content they share on LinkedIn and to see who is engaging with that content as well. These updates will show up in your LinkedIn news feed.

To source new connections from company pages, you can either visit the page directly or use LinkedIn's advanced search.

One idea is to conduct a search for a specific company. J.C. Penney is a large company that is headquartered in my city. I created an advanced LinkedIn search for my zip code to search for 1st- and 2nd-degree connections, as well as mutual group members who currently work at J.C. Penney. I also added the keyword "Manager" so that my search results would only show managers from J.C. Penney.

This search returned over five hundred results. I reviewed this list of professionals for shared connections and began selectively sending invitations to connect.

Don't overlook company data on LinkedIn. You can find highly relevant people to grow your network with through company pages and searches.

Connect through Content Engagement

Your LinkedIn homepage news feed is full of updates from the activities of your network members. Status updates of articles and images are being shared. Those members you follow are publishing new posts to the LinkedIn Publishing Platform. Group discussions are being highlighted as well.

You can engage with any of these updates in your news feed by liking, sharing, or commenting on them. You may also uncover out-of-network people to connect with who are also engaging with the updates in your news feed.

I have found some very interesting people to connect with just by getting involved in conversations around a popular news feed item. In order to get involved in a conversation, simply post a comment on the update.

This same concept applies to LinkedIn group discussions. When you engage in conversations on LinkedIn, you open the door to making new, relevant connections.

Build Your Smart Network On The Go

Did you know that 50 percent of LinkedIn's traffic comes from mobile? That is a staggering statistic. If you are not using LinkedIn's mobile apps, you are missing a big opportunity to grow and engage with your network.

LinkedIn has two mobile apps that can help you build your smart network on the go.

The primary LinkedIn mobile app really includes much of the same functionality as the desktop version of LinkedIn. With this app, you can conduct searches and send invitations to connect.

In order to personalize your invitation from the primary mobile app, you will need to look for the small menu icon at the top of the profile you are viewing. There you will see an option to customize your invitation. Otherwise, if you just click the big blue "connect" button, you will send a generic invitation.

The other LinkedIn mobile app is called *Connected*. Through the *Connected* app, you can connect with the "people you may know" that LinkedIn highlights for you. Customize your invitation by clicking on the small menu icon versus clicking on the large "+" sign. You will just need to look closely for that menu icon.

I'll talk more about how to use the LinkedIn *Connected* app later in the book.

LinkedIn's mobile apps can keep you plugged in on the go and assist you in growing your network in just a few minutes a day.

What Are Followers and Do They Matter?

You may be aware that you can earn followers now on LinkedIn just like you can on Twitter and other social networks. The number of followers shown on your profile includes your 1st-degree connections, as well as unconnected followers. Anyone on LinkedIn can follow you without actually connecting with you and becoming a part of your 1st-degree network. You can also follow anyone on LinkedIn.

Your followers will be able to see and engage with your published posts on LinkedIn, but they won't see anything else that is not public information.

Growing your followers is a great way to grow your reach on LinkedIn. The best way to grow your followers is to publish posts on LinkedIn's built-in publishing platform. I cover this strategy in Rule #7.

Encouraging people to follow you that you don't want to officially connect with can also keep you on track with building your smart network.

Use Discretion When Accepting LinkedIn Invitations

Once you know with whom you should be connecting on LinkedIn to build a smarter network, it becomes pretty clear whom not to connect with.

I have a few additional suggestions to help you with this:

- Don't accept invitations from people who are missing a primary profile image
- Don't accept invitations from people who have an unusual or unprofessional profile image (I've seen someone use a dog's head as their profile image!)
- Don't accept invitations from people whose profiles don't seem legitimate (you will know when you see them; there are quite a few fake profiles out there)
- Use discretion when accepting an invitation that is not personalized, especially from someone you do not know

- Always look for a common thread that is consistent with your *unique market opportunities* before accepting an invitation

One way to determine whether or not a new connection request is viable is to review the connections you have in common. If you see familiar faces as shared connections, it is probably okay to accept the invitation.

Remember, you can always suggest that someone follow you on LinkedIn rather than allowing them into your 1st-degree network.

There have been a number of incidents where I have accepted an invitation from someone I did not know, and they sent me a sales pitch message soon after on LinkedIn. I immediately remove people like that from my connections.

When you send invitations on LinkedIn, make sure you are not doing any of the above! Send a personalized invitation any time that you can. Remember, it will stand out, and the receiver will be more likely to accept.

Make Smart Network Building a Top Priority

I can't emphasize enough how important your LinkedIn network is today and how important it will be to you in the future. Being smart about the way you build your LinkedIn network is critical to attracting and building personal influence with the right clients.

Building your LinkedIn network is also not a one-time event. It's an ongoing activity. You should focus on expanding and improving your network daily. This includes pruning your network and removing those connections that you once said yes to but today may no longer be relevant.

With a precise profile and smart network in place, you are ready for the next level! In the following chapters, I'm going to teach you more about how to grow your personal influence with your network.

Chapter 3

RULE #3—Grow Your Visibility through Value

> *The essence of strategy is in activities—choosing to perform activities differently or to perform different activities than rivals.*
>
> - Michael E. Porter

In the digital age, we are bombarded with so many online messages and posts that it is impossible to keep up. It is imperative in today's noisy world not only to be visible with your ideal clients, but also to be valuable—so valuable that your ideal clients will seek you out. You can become their beacon of light and voice of reason!

Is it possible to stand out like this and rise above the noise? Is it possible to have your ideal clients or customers searching specifically for you and readily consuming every piece of content you share? Absolutely. This is the result of building your personal influence.

LinkedIn is an ideal platform for giving value to the most important people in your professional world. It is also not terribly difficult to stand out on LinkedIn, even if you increase your activity level just slightly. Visibility plus value is a powerful combination.

It is true that the more active you are on LinkedIn, the more visible you will be with your network. But the value you give to your network to help them overcome challenges and improve their lives is what will grow your personal influence.

You should always be more focused on the needs and desires of your LinkedIn connections than on your own objectives.

Build Your Network Influence with LinkedIn Status Updates

Sharing status updates on LinkedIn is the easiest way to stay active, visible, and valuable with your network. Sharing value consistently on LinkedIn can keep you top of mind with your network and position you as an influencer in your market, niche, or industry.

Activities such as participating in group discussions, making new connections, following companies, and engaging in updates from your network are also ways to create visibility on LinkedIn. However, I'm primarily going to have you focus on the activity of sharing *status updates*.

Did you realize that someone must see you online seven to ten times before they remember you? If you aren't giving value each time you share something on LinkedIn, you may not get another chance. Share your best ideas and insights along with the best content you can find. Don't hold back.

Status updates are short posts you can share with your LinkedIn network at any time. These short posts can include text, images, a link, a video, and even a slide presentation. Your status updates can be liked, shared, or commented on by your 1st-degree connections and your extended network as well.

Your status updates may or may not always be seen by your connections. This is due to LinkedIn's algorithm of customizing and personalizing the news feeds of members. In order for your status updates to be seen, they need to be worthy of engagement by the members of your network. Your updates need to be valuable, informative, and helpful in order to attract engagement.

Your posting schedule can also be a factor for engagement. If you are posting status updates in the middle of the night, you won't get the same level of traction that you might during the workday. (More on timing shortly.)

When members of your network see you frequently sharing valuable status updates on LinkedIn that are meaningful to them, they are going to naturally be inclined to learn more about you, what you do, who you work with, and what your interests are. More of your connections will view your profile, visit your website, and even contact you directly.

Remember, personal influence amplifies everything that you do on LinkedIn. As your personal influence grows, you will not have to spend as much time and effort on your LinkedIn activities. *Your influence will do the work for you.* Each status update you share will have greater impact.

Understand Who You Are Connected To

Once you have done the work of improving your network to make it smarter, you will have a better understanding of who you are connected to on LinkedIn. Knowing your network better makes sharing relevant information that much easier.

None of us has a "pure" network. Our networks consist of network clusters. Understanding who makes up the majority of your LinkedIn network is important because you want to share status updates that resonate with your network!

One way to better understand your network is to conduct an advanced LinkedIn search of your 1st-degree connections and filter for "All" under the industry filter. This search will give you a breakdown of your network by industry.

Once you understand the industries represented by your network, you can better target your status updates to be value-added. Industry-specific status updates may make a lot of sense if your network is made up mostly of a single industry.

In my case, the majority of my connections work in the financial services industry, or in professional services such as legal, accounting, and consulting. There is also a significant segment of professionals in my network who work in the digital marketing industry.

My goal, then, is to share valuable status updates that resonate across *all* of these industries. These are the updates that tend to get the best engagement from my network.

Post Universal Status Updates

What if your LinkedIn network consists of multiple industries?

Consider sharing *universal* content with your network. Think more about what all entrepreneurs and business professionals want and struggle with *collectively*.

Most entrepreneurs and business professionals want to know how to grow their businesses, become more productive, enhance credibility, gain knowledge and expertise, expand their influence, become better leaders, make more money, improve their lives, be inspired, improve their energy levels, reduce stress, find talent, grow their networks, and the list goes on! These are what I refer to as *universal* themes that apply to all entrepreneurs and business professionals.

Appealing to a broader audience with your status updates may increase your engagement levels more than sharing industry-specific content.

The higher your engagement levels on your status updates, the greater your visibility will be. The more visible you are, the more memorable and influential you can become to your network.

It is also very possible to appeal to a narrower segment of your network with industry-specific status updates.

Going back to the example of my network, I could share updates that only appeal to the segment of my network working in the financial services industry and still gain traction in the news feed.

Unfortunately, there is no way to target your status updates from your personal LinkedIn profile. However, LinkedIn's news feed algorithm is getting smarter about personalizing the news feed for each member.

The best thing to do is experiment and test. See which of your status updates are receiving the most likes, shares, and comments. Regardless of what information you decide to share with your network, make sure you are adding as much value as possible. I can't stress this enough.

Ultimately, engagement with your network is the key to earning visibility in the LinkedIn news feed!

Personalize Your LinkedIn Status Updates to Increase Engagement

The ultimate goal with your status updates is to earn *engagement* from your network. You want your connections to like, share, and comment on your updates. Achieving higher engagement levels with your updates will also teach LinkedIn that you share good stuff with your network. These are the updates LinkedIn likes to show in the news feed.

In Rule #1, I covered how important it is to personalize your LinkedIn profile. It is equally important to personalize your LinkedIn status updates. This means sprinkling in your *personality*, *passion*, and *perspective* whenever possible. Personalization will help you achieve higher engagement levels with your status updates.

Jeff Goins of Tribe Writers shared a story with me about Stephen King. He said that the common thread through all of Stephen King's books is not that they are horror novels. (They are not all horror novels, actually.)

The common thread through Stephen King's novels is that his blue-collar upbringing clearly shines through. His background has influenced his perspective. Think about your perspective. How do you see the world and how can you convey your perspective through your LinkedIn status updates?

You can easily weave your personality, passion, and perspective into your status updates by including a personal comment or question each time you share. As of the time of this writing, LinkedIn status updates can contain up to six hundred characters.

Examples of personalizing your updates include sharing your thoughts, opinions, or personal tidbits about yourself to enhance your status updates.

For example, one time I shared an article on LinkedIn about how the practice of yoga can benefit your business. Given that I practice yoga frequently and am very passionate about it, I included a comment about how powerful the practice of yoga has been for improving my business.

Making that personal connection with your network is what really fosters engagement.

How many updates in your LinkedIn news feed do you see that are not personalized? Most LinkedIn members aren't taking the time to infuse their personalities into their status updates. They are simply blasting out content, much of it being overtly promotional!

Being more personable and authentic with your LinkedIn status updates will drive engagement and help your connections better understand who you are, how you think, and what you believe in. Personalization builds personal influence.

Be Consistently Active...

Nearly every activity you engage in on LinkedIn creates a visible update that can potentially be seen by your network.

When you post a status update, contribute to a group discussion, publish a long-form post, make a new connection, follow a company or a publisher, and like, share, or comment on posts, these actions can be visible to your network. (Updating your LinkedIn profile also creates a visible action unless you turn this off in your settings.)

Consistency builds trust. If you aren't consistently active on LinkedIn, you will be out of mind. Your connections are not going to think of you first if they aren't seeing you frequently. Furthermore, if your competitors are more active on LinkedIn than you are, this can hurt your business.

Being consistently active on LinkedIn will earn you what I call **network mindshare**.

If you are consistently active in earning **network mindshare** on LinkedIn, your connections are going to think of you first when they need help or someone they know needs help.

I can't tell you how many of my current clients said to me in our initial business discussions, "I see you on LinkedIn all the time." Staying top of mind with your LinkedIn network works, and most LinkedIn members have a tough time being consistent. You can be the one to earn the majority of **network mindshare** and stand out with your network!

...But Don't Over-Share

LinkedIn has suggested that twenty status updates per month can reach 60 percent of your unique audience (that would be one status update per weekday). Given the news feed algorithm update, this may not continue to be the case.

Over-sharing occurs when you are posting too many status updates on LinkedIn and some of your connections begin to hide you from their news feeds. This does happen! I have hidden a good number of my connections because they either post too much, or what they post isn't valuable.

Another common practice I see is that some LinkedIn members have another individual deciding what to post for them. These posts are not personalized and many times are overtly self-promotional while lacking in value.

At the very least, you should be the one deciding what gets posted to your LinkedIn network. This is your professional reputation, after all!

If you post a valuable LinkedIn status update no more than twice a day, this is probably a healthy frequency. If you don't seem to be getting any engagement on your updates, increase your frequency. If you still are not getting engagement, you are most likely not sharing valuable enough information.

Seek to inform with your status updates, but also seek to inspire.

The Practice of Proximity on LinkedIn

The practice of proximity is sharing the right messages with the right people at the right time(s). It is difficult to achieve all three of these with your LinkedIn status updates, which is why I refer to it as a *practice*. Proximity is both an art and a science.

Remember, it may work best for you to share status updates with your network that highlight the common problems and desires that they face in growing their business or careers. I'll focus on *what* to share more specifically in the remainder of this chapter.

When to share status updates is more difficult to decipher. LinkedIn doesn't provide much insight into the number of views your status updates receive other than the most recent one you've completed. I suspect this will be going away altogether at some point.

What you can see is the level of engagement, which is much more valuable than views. You can see the likes, shares, and comments that your status updates receive.

To determine the best times and days to share status updates, you will need to experiment and see which updates are getting more engagement.

I recommend posting status updates to LinkedIn at different times, both day and night, in order to determine what works best for you.

The right *timing* of a status update can also help you achieve significant engagement.

An example of great timing is when *Content Marketing Institute* shared a video post of highlights of a Kevin Spacey keynote from their most recent conference on the same day that his wildly popular series *House of Cards* launched a new season on Netflix.

Think about current news and events you can share to get your network engaged. Make sure you are adding value in the process by explaining how these current happenings are relevant to your connections!

Leverage LinkedIn Pulse

LinkedIn Pulse is a powerful and professional content hub that lives on LinkedIn. Here you can easily discover high-quality content to share with your network. Essentially, LinkedIn is doing the aggregating and curating for you.

The best way to keep tabs on content that would be relevant to you is to follow the official LinkedIn Influencers, topical channels, and media publishers on *LinkedIn Pulse.*

When you follow these sources on LinkedIn, you will see their published posts in your news feed. Look for posts that are achieving high levels of engagement (comments, likes, shares) to share with your network!

Click the LinkedIn "share" button on any post you want to share. You will see a box where you can customize your message and even publicly @mention the author of the post by name. (Normally you can only @mention a 1st-degree connection.)

For the time being, it appears as though you can @mention *anyone* who has published a Pulse post on LinkedIn. This is a great way to publicly promote the author of the post and get on his or her radar!

LinkedIn Pulse is also available as a mobile app. Not only can you discover timely and valuable content through this app, you can share these curated articles from your device with your network in one click.

Checking in on the *Pulse* mobile app is something I do each morning to start my day. I especially pay attention to the content that is trending in my network and look for interesting and valuable updates to share.

Consider Using Status Update Formats That Work Well

Some status updates will perform better than others based on their format! Below are a few ideas to consider with your updates:

Ask a question — Asking questions on LinkedIn invites your connections to comment. People love to give their answers and feedback.

Share links to articles — Link posts will pull in an image, title, and description from the original article.

(*Note:* When you share videos from YouTube, presentations from SlideShare, and even podcasts from SoundCloud, each of these will automatically create an image with your status update.)

Share image-based posts — When you upload an image to your status update (you are still able to include some introductory text and a link), the image item will appear much larger in the news feed than it would if you simply allowed LinkedIn to pull in the image for the article you are sharing.

Share videos and slide decks — YouTube videos and SlideShare slide decks that are shared as status updates will show up more prominently in the news feed. They will also be viewable within the LinkedIn news feed.

With every update you share on LinkedIn, don't forget to personalize with your own comments!

Share Your Own Content

One of the key components to building your personal influence is by revealing how well you understand the needs and desires of your ideal clients or customers. Sharing your message through the content you create is perfectly acceptable if it truly adds value and can help the members of your network get smarter, solve a problem, or achieve more of what they want.

Be careful about sharing updates that overtly promote your products or services. If you do promote a free offer, such as an educational guide or webinar, you should do so thoughtfully and strategically.

The more effective method for ultimately selling your products or services is to give as much knowledge and guidance away to your network as possible. Not only does this method establish your credibility, it also provides value.

If you are creating blog posts, podcasts, and/or videos that teach something valuable, I absolutely recommend sharing that content with your network.

Top influencers promote their own content. You can only get into trouble with this if your content is *selling*. Building your personal influence will take care of all of your selling in the long run.

I recommend sharing your own content anywhere from 25 percent to 50 percent of the time on LinkedIn, depending on how much content you produce.

Sharing articles from third-party sources where you have been featured or interviewed can also work well. In this case, you are involved in the piece but not the original contributor or creator.

It's also okay to share existing content that you have created more than once with your network. Simply spread out your timing on recycled status updates and change up your introductory text.

Consider repurposing existing content into different formats and share again.

For example, I've published a podcast that I had transcribed into a blog post. The first time I shared this content, I shared the audio podcast directly from SoundCloud, where it could be easily accessed by my network. The second time I shared this content, I shared the actual blog post from my website, which included a written summary of that same audio podcast.

Creating and sharing different formats of your content can also help you appeal to more members of your network. We each have our own preferences for the types of content we like to consume, whether it is in written, audio, or video form.

Post Status Updates to Twitter Simultaneously

If you connect Twitter to your LinkedIn account, you can post a status update to both your LinkedIn network and Twitter followers at the same time.

Keep in mind that you are limited to 140 characters for a tweet while a LinkedIn status update can include up to 700 characters. Anything beyond the 140 characters for Twitter will be truncated.

This is a simple strategy for being more efficient with your time!

Participate in Group Discussions

Group discussions are ideal for sharing more of your subject-matter expertise in the form of answering questions, giving feedback, and pointing to valuable resources across the social web. Your group participation also posts to the news feeds of your LinkedIn connections.

You can build your personal influence within groups while also showcasing your participation to your network. This is another great way to create "passive" visibility with your network and potentially get some of your connections engaged in the conversation.

I go into great detail about how to leverage LinkedIn groups in Rule #6.

Use the @mention Feature in Your Status Updates

The @mention feature provides an opportunity for you to publicly recognize any of your 1st-degree LinkedIn connections in your status updates. This feature works extremely well for building your influence, and it is underutilized. The @mention feature is one of my favorite tools for building personal influence with important people on LinkedIn.

The person or people you @mention in a status update will be notified by LinkedIn in an e-mail. This encourages the person you @mention to engage with your post. (I've rarely had someone not engage with my status update when tagging him or her with an @mention.)

When you share a post that one of your network members has published or shared, @mention them in your status update. Typically, it makes sense to frame your @mention in the form of a compliment.

For example, I shared a blog post published by an influential 1st-degree connection. In my status update, I tagged him with an @mention. Most important, I included a comment about why I believed his article was so valuable.

Not only was my 1st-degree LinkedIn connection flattered that I had mentioned him, but he was very appreciative of my words. When you use an @mention in this way, you must be genuine and sincere.

You can also @mention anyone who has published an article on LinkedIn's publishing platform, whether or not you are connected to them. I recommend clicking the LinkedIn "share" button to share the article with your network. Here you can customize your message and @mention the author of the article! Want to get on an Influencer's radar? This is the way to do it.

Another way to leverage the @mention feature is to stay informed about your 1st-degree connections. *Newsle* is a killer software application owned by LinkedIn that you can sign up for, and it's free (visit www.newsle.com). Newsle will analyze your LinkedIn connections and send you e-mail alerts any time one of your connections publishes new content online or is mentioned in the news.

I frequently will share the articles that Newsle sends me about the people in my network and include an @mention for my connection in the status update.

Engage with Status Updates Posted by Your Network

A simple way to stay highly visible and valuable on LinkedIn without having to constantly come up with your own ideas to share is to engage with the status updates posted by your network.

Whenever you like, share, or comment on someone else's status update, this activity can be just as visible to your network as if it were your own update.

There is another significant benefit to engaging with the status updates from your network. It gives you the chance to build rapport with the person who has shared the update. It is a subtle way to acknowledge, promote, and even give feedback, or start a conversation through commenting on the post.

You may be wondering if it is better to like, share, or comment on status updates. This depends on the update. For example, one of my connections published an insightful article for marketers who run digital agencies. I liked the update and also left a comment to acknowledge his work, but it wasn't relevant to share with my entire network.

When you share someone else's status update, you have the ability to add your own commentary as well.

You could decide to like, share, and comment on the same status update if you wanted to. All three of these actions will show up in the news feeds of your network. Also, the person who posted the update will be notified of your actions.

The engagement action that gets the most traction is a share. When you share someone's status update, your personalized text shows up at the top of the update. In a sense, you take ownership of the content while still giving credit to the person who originally posted the update.

Whenever you engage with a status update in your news feed, the person who posted the update will be notified by LinkedIn. Depending on their notification settings, members can receive e-mails each time you like, share, or comment on one of their updates.

Engaging with status updates posted by your LinkedIn connections is an easy way to stay active, strengthen relationships, and build influence simultaneously.

LinkedIn Notification Settings

In order to be notified about the engagement happening with your network, make sure to review your notification settings on LinkedIn.

Visit your "Privacy & Settings" area and look for "push notification settings." Customize these settings to receive notifications when LinkedIn members engage with your status updates, @mention you, follow you, like your group discussions, and more. You will receive these notifications via e-mail, and they will also show up under the flag icon at the top of your LinkedIn homepage.

If the e-mail notifications get too overwhelming, you can always uncheck some of the boxes within your push notification settings.

It is most effective to respond quickly to engagement that happens around your activity on LinkedIn versus responding several days later or not knowing about it at all.

LinkedIn Tools for Increasing Your Efficiency

LinkedIn's primary mobile app is a great tool for engaging with updates from your network on the go. You can keep up with what's happening in your LinkedIn news feed, and you can post status updates from the app.

You can also participate in group discussions and quickly engage with status updates from your network. You can conduct searches, make new connections, and see who has been viewing your profile. The LinkedIn mobile app is invaluable for networking and engaging on the go.

LinkedIn's Pulse mobile app works best for sourcing interesting, insightful, and inspirational content to share with your network. You can also comment on any of the Pulse articles from the mobile app.

If you want to save time with posting status updates to LinkedIn, I recommend using a tool like <u>Buffer</u>. With Buffer, you can preload the status updates you want to share and have them post according to a schedule that you set up. This allows you to share content when it would be most effective rather than when you find it. For example, if you find valuable links to content you want to share with your network in the middle of the night, you can add them to Buffer and schedule them to post the next day.

There is a caveat to using third-party tools to manage your LinkedIn status updates. The connection between LinkedIn and third-party tools tends to break more often than it does with other social networks. That means you have to reauthorize your LinkedIn account from time to time to reconnect it with the outside tool.

Also, when posting status updates to LinkedIn from third-party tools, images may not resolve correctly in the news feeds of your connections. Always double check how your updates look to others by reviewing your LinkedIn activity screen (accessible from your homepage).

The fastest way to start growing your visibility and influence with your network on LinkedIn is by adding value through your status updates. When you become consistently visible and valuable, you will build greater personal influence with your network.

Now that you understand how to effectively become more active on LinkedIn, it's time to learn how to take it to the next level and start networking smarter!

Chapter 4

RULE #4: Network Smarter

> *You can have everything you want in life if you will just help enough other people get what they want.*
>
> - Zig Ziglar

When I began my career with a major financial firm in 1995, I was charged with finding new clients who would invest their retirement assets with me. My boss gave me a cubicle to sit in, a telephone, and a White Pages phone book. The basic instructions I received were to "smile and dial" for new prospects.

There is nothing more miserable than having to cold-call strangers at dinnertime. It is dreadful. I knew right away that I would have to figure out another way to meet prospective clients. I found that networking was the best way to meet my ideal clients and build relationships with them.

Although networking worked well back in those days, it still took months and sometimes years to develop the high level of trust required for someone to ultimately do business with me.

LinkedIn has changed professional networking *forever*. It is a virtual, global, professional networking event that is going on twenty-four hours a day, seven days a week. We can connect and converse with people on LinkedIn in minutes, not hours. We can also narrow down our networking on LinkedIn to focus on our niches and local cities and towns. LinkedIn accelerates and scales the relationship-building process like never before.

The majority of LinkedIn members are there to build their professional networks, stay informed, grow their visibility, and find business or career opportunities. Your goal with LinkedIn networking is simple. It is to help the members of your network get what they need and want! This is networking *smarter*.

Let me explain. Networking smarter requires a paradigm shift. You don't have to ever promote your business when you are networking smarter. Instead, your role is to go into LinkedIn and search for opportunities to guide and serve your network members. What do they need? What do they want? Who do they need to know? What will make them look good to their networks?

Do you see the difference? Good. Let's move forward.

Get Them in Your 1st-Degree Network

The best way to guide and serve others on LinkedIn is to get the right people into your network. This is why building a smarter network on LinkedIn is so critical. For a refresher on how to build a smarter network, go back and review Chapter 2 (Rule #2).

When you invite a new person into your 1st-degree network, you gain more information about them. The more you know about someone, the easier it is to connect them with the right people and opportunities.

You also gain greater access to your 1st-degree connections. You can have a one-to-one dialogue with them through LinkedIn messaging and accelerate the relationship-building process.

If your 1st-degree connections make their connections public, you can learn who they are connected to and the connections you have in common with them.

Higher-quality networking is more achievable with your 1st-degree network. Networking outside of this circle can take place, as well, it is just a little more difficult and, most of the time, requires that you have a premium LinkedIn account (which I do recommend).

Be a Giver on LinkedIn

The simple secret to getting what you want is giving others what they want. When you genuinely give to others to help them solve a problem, improve, get smarter, or expand their network on LinkedIn, it will come back to you. You will trigger the *Rule of Reciprocity*.

When the *Rule of Reciprocity* is triggered, the people you help will feel some level of obligation to help you in return. However, there is a catch. The catch is that you must be genuine and authentic in your giving. You must sincerely feel it and mean it. You also must expect nothing in return.

When you become a giver on LinkedIn, you will spend your time on activities such as promoting, acknowledging, thanking, endorsing, congratulating, sharing, asking, conversing, introducing, referring, and connecting others.

Here is a story about the power of giving on LinkedIn. One of my 1st-degree connections sent me a LinkedIn message asking for my help. Let's call him Dan (not his real name). Dan believed that someone I was connected with on LinkedIn would be the perfect client for him. Dan asked in his LinkedIn message if I could refer him to this individual.

This made me uncomfortable, as it would most people. I didn't really know Dan that well yet, and I was pretty sure that my contact did not need the services he was offering. My response to Dan was to say that I knew my contact was already taken care of in this area, but that I would keep my eyes and ears open for him.

Several weeks later, I heard from Dan again. This time, he did something very different. Instead of asking me to refer him to someone I knew, he gave me a referral. Not only that, but Dan set up the referral relationship perfectly by providing me with contact information and stating, "She will be expecting your call." All I had to do was call and initiate contact with this referral.

The referral Dan sent to me through LinkedIn ended up becoming a client. Now, I go above and beyond to send Dan introductions and referrals whenever I can.

The moral of the story? *Give to earn.* When you genuinely give something of value without ever asking for anything in return, you will earn that value back. You will have triggered the *Rule of Reciprocity.*

Leverage the 80/20 Pareto Principle

You may be familiar with the Pareto Principle, which says that 80 percent of your results come from 20 percent of your actions. The Pareto Principle can be leveraged throughout your entire LinkedIn presence.

- Twenty percent of your actions on LinkedIn will produce 80 percent of your results
- Twenty percent of your time spent on LinkedIn will produce 80 percent of your results
- Twenty percent of your network will produce 80 percent of your results

I am a huge fan of leveraging the Pareto Principle on LinkedIn. By using the 80/20 rule, you will narrow your networking focus. This will save you time, effort, and energy, and help you achieve your desired results more quickly.

Networking activities on LinkedIn are not created equal. There are certain networking activities that have a greater impact than others. These are the 20 percent "networking smarter" activities that I will be focusing on in this chapter.

You will also want to identify your **MVCs** (Most Valuable Connections) on LinkedIn. Your MVCs might include clients or customers, prospects, decision-makers, professional partners, referral sources, industry leaders and influencers, journalists, and your most loyal advocates.

I will share more about focusing on your MVCs shortly. For now, just understand that your MVCs are the most important people in your network. Spending your LinkedIn networking time with these individuals will accelerate your success.

Networking smarter on LinkedIn is really about focusing on the right people with the right actions. When you do this, you save time, energy, and effort.

Gather Intelligence about the People in Your Network

One of the major advantages of social networks and the Internet is that you can learn personal and professional details about any of the connections you make online. Having access to these details can help you find common connection points for starting conversations, nurturing relationships, and serving the people you are connected to.

Reid Hoffman, cofounder and executive chairman of LinkedIn, refers to being intelligent about your network as being "network literate." Hoffman says that we've moved from the Information Age to the Networked Age and that a major part of the process to becoming *network literate* is utilizing network technology and intelligence.[5]

A key to successful networking on LinkedIn is gathering intelligence about those you want to connect with and those you are already connected with. When you learn more about people, you can leverage your common connection points to strengthen the relationship.

I have a financial advisor friend who landed a new client because they saw on one of her social media profiles that she loved to snow ski! This is a true story. Common connection points can create instant bonds with people.

This also means you have to showcase the things you care about and enjoy on social networks, including LinkedIn. Share as much information about yourself as you are comfortable with. Of course, you don't ever want to get too personal. Just share the

---

[5] Reid Hoffman Blog: http://reidhoffman.org/information-age-networked-age-network-literate

things that can connect you with others who are similar to you or have things in common with you.

The power of your network is only as strong as your knowledge about the people within your network. Understanding their needs, goals, dreams, passions, and challenges is critical to adding value to their personal and professional lives.

Engage in "Five-Minute" LinkedIn Favors

A key difference between offline networking and online social networking is the ability to engage in quick but meaningful actions that increase your influence with others. You can actually engage in helping your network members with small favors, in small increments of time, and still be highly effective.

Adam Grant, author of *Give and Take*, calls these actions *five-minute favors*. The idea of five-minute favors is to add high value to the lives of others at a low personal cost. You don't have to invest substantial time and energy to help and serve others on social networks like LinkedIn.

These small digital favors for others can differentiate you and position you as a valuable resource to your network.

Examples of five-minute LinkedIn favors might include connecting two people together who can benefit from meeting, sharing a valuable resource, or sending a private LinkedIn message that provides feedback or assistance. You can even give a five-minute favor through posting an answer or recommendation within a LinkedIn group discussion.

To make this strategy work, you want to keenly observe your network and listen to them within LinkedIn and outside of LinkedIn. Look for opportunities to answer questions, solve problems, or provide an actual resource.

When networking on LinkedIn, constantly be on the lookout for these *five-minute favor* opportunities.

Notice (and Act) on the Little Things

LinkedIn makes it easy for you to stay updated on some of the little things happening with your network. Are you noticing?

Make sure to subscribe to the **LinkedIn Updates** e-mail (you can turn these e-mails on in your LinkedIn "Privacy & Settings"). LinkedIn will send you a customized daily e-mail about the members of your network who are having birthdays, work anniversaries, job changes, or "in the news" appearances.

Another way to get these updates is through the LinkedIn *Connected* app. This is the mobile app I covered in Chapter 2 (Rule #2) that can help you quickly scan through these opportunities on a daily basis. You can send short, personalized messages to your connections directly from the app!

These small gestures of acknowledgement may not seem like a big deal, but they are. They give you the opportunity to stay top of mind with your connections on an individual basis, and it lets them know you are paying attention. Most LinkedIn members don't bother to notice or act on these small events.

Become a Connection Specialist on LinkedIn

Connecting two people together by making an introduction or referral is one of the most effective ways to build your network influence. It also allows you to help two people at the same time.

Getting to know your 1st-degree connections better can help tremendously with making relevant introductions. I suggest starting by making a few lists of important connections that you can study and learn more about.

Starting with the people in your network who you already know well makes the process of finding valuable introductions to make easier. Make a list of your clients, your strategic partners, and the top influencers in your network. You can tag these individuals accordingly and also record private notes about them within LinkedIn. (You could also do this using your own Client Relationship Manager [CRM] tool.)

Use LinkedIn's advanced search tool to find your 1st-degree connections who live in the same location, work in the same industry, and share the same interests (use keywords to find common interests in your searches).

For example, I've conducted a search of my 1st-degree connections who work in Dallas and have an interest in golf. That search returned over four hundred results! Think about all of the introductions I could make just based on these common connection points. I could also invite a group out to play golf and make introductions.

You can initiate an introduction between two people on LinkedIn by sharing their profiles. Simply visit the LinkedIn profile of the person you would like to introduce and click "Share Profile." A prewritten message will appear for you to type in the name of your connection you want to forward it to. You will be able to customize this message and explain why you are making the introduction.

Unfortunately, this method is a bit confusing. If you do share a profile through LinkedIn along with a message, you might follow up to help them actually get connected on LinkedIn or communicate via e-mail.

Ideally, if you can introduce two people through e-mail, it is a little less confusing than the LinkedIn system.

Become a Master at the "Circle-and-Fill" Method

Another way to figure out who to connect together is to use the "circle-and-fill" method. This smart networking method can really catapult your influence with your MVCs. *Circle* your MVCs and *fill* any professional gaps they have with a qualified referral that can help them.

First, ask your MVC whom they work with and recommend for various professional services: a lawyer, accountant, mortgage broker, realtor, doctor, interior designer, homebuilder, insurance agent, and financial advisor are examples. Let your MVC know that you would love to get connected with these professionals (on

LinkedIn), and that your clients often need these kinds of services as well.

Typically, your MVCs will be happy to share the names of the professional services providers they work with and recommend. Connect with these providers on LinkedIn to build rapport. Be sure to ask the permission of your MVC to use his or her name, and provide context to the professional provider as to why you would like to connect on LinkedIn.

As you go through this process with each of your MVCs, you will surface relevant professionals to connect with that you can potentially refer business to. You will also identify the "gaps" with each of your MVCs and be able to fill those gaps with qualified referrals.

For example, some of your contacts might be looking for an architect, dentist, or personal trainer. Others will already have these slots filled by someone they trust. Your job is to find and fill in the gaps by making relevant referrals to your MVCs where they are needed.

Whenever you make a referral, let both your MVC and the professional services provider know that you have done so.

What you will find with this smart networking exercise is that your MVCs will appreciate being asked about whom they recommend and they will value your help in filling their professional-service gaps.

Additionally, you will make new connections with qualified professionals who work with people just like your clients or customers, and you will potentially be able to refer them new business.

The circle-and-fill networking method is one of the greatest ways to make highly relevant connections and help the people who are most important to your business. It is one of my top secrets for networking success.

Develop Strategic Partnerships

Developing strategic partnerships with select LinkedIn connections is similar to some of the above strategies I've shared with you.

A strategic partner is someone who is already in front of your target market, providing a noncompeting service. Strategic partners can also be influencers in your industry.

By connecting on LinkedIn and building relationships with strategic partners, you can help grow their visibility and influence with your network, and they can help you grow your visibility and influence with their networks. It is a win-win.

Promote your strategic partners to your network on LinkedIn. Introduce them to key people in your network. Endorse their skills and expertise. Give them a written recommendation on LinkedIn. Share their content with your network on LinkedIn. Refer them clients. Refer them for speaking opportunities and media or podcast interviews.

When you develop these strategic partnerships and foster them on LinkedIn, you can become visible and valuable way beyond your 1st-degree network. You can become known to hundreds, if not thousands, of people in your target audience who already trust the people who have partnered with you.

Once you establish a relationship with a partner by getting them into your network on LinkedIn, you can explore joint-venture projects that will benefit both of your target audiences.

What really helps in making strategic partnerships work is clearly communicating on your LinkedIn profile exactly what you do and whom you help. When you specialize in a market or niche area of expertise, you open up more strategic partnering opportunities.

Showcase and Promote Your Connections Using LinkedIn @mentions

I touched on using @mentions in LinkedIn status updates in the last chapter. The real value of @mentions, though, is utilizing them to *network* publicly with your 1st-degree connections.

With @mentions, you can publicly recognize and promote your 1st-degree connections to your network. You can also start public conversations with @mentions.

When you are posting a LinkedIn status update or comment, you can tag a 1st-degree connection (or multiple 1st-degree connections) in your update by using the "@" symbol immediately followed by the name of the person (or company) you are mentioning. The @mention will be linked to their actual LinkedIn profile. They will also receive an e-mail and a notification on LinkedIn that you've mentioned them in your update.

Many times, when you use an @mention, the person you mention will engage with your update once they have received notification. When this happens, your update can also be visible to their connections.

You can also @mention companies in your updates or comments. The @mention will be directly linked to the company's LinkedIn page. Your @mention will show up in the notification section of the company's LinkedIn page. This can come in handy if you are looking to get on the radar of a particular company.

Use @mentions to promote your 1st-degree connections to share content where they have been mentioned in the news, quoted, or interviewed.

Here is a creative way I have used an @mention to make a strategic connection: I had written about a high-level executive in my industry in a blog article. I wanted to share the article on LinkedIn with my network and @mention her, but we weren't connected at the 1st-degree level.

First, I crafted an InMail (a paid LinkedIn feature) and sent her a message to tell her about the blog post and included a link for her to review it. I explained how I wanted to share the blog post with my network and mention her publicly, but we had to be 1st-degree connections on LinkedIn for me to do so. I asked her if she would be okay with me sending her an invitation to connect.

Not only did she agree to connect, but she was flattered that I had spoken highly of her in my blog article. I promoted the article through a status update on LinkedIn and @mentioned her. She engaged with a public "thank you," which meant that some of her network members also saw the update. Additionally, a few members of her LinkedIn network commented on the update.

Can you see the networking power of a single @mention?

You can also @mention multiple 1st-degree connections in a single status update. A number of my younger peers were recognized for their innovation and written up in an online industry publication. I shared that article with my network, congratulating those who were recognized, and I @mentioned those with whom I was connected.

There are many creative ways to use LinkedIn @mentions for networking.

Give Endorsements and Recommendations

I covered endorsements extensively in Chapter 1 (Rule #1) for powering up your LinkedIn profile. Giving endorsements is also a form of networking.

When you give an endorsement to one of your connections for their specific skills and expertise, they will be notified and have the ability to publish your endorsement on their profile.

Endorsements are a good example of a five-minute favor. People appreciate them, and when you give endorsements, you typically will get them in return.

LinkedIn does a nice job of prompting you to endorse your 1st-degree connections. You will see these prompts frequently, especially when you go to endorse one of your connections. However, I have found that you need to take a few minutes from time to time to go through and endorse some of your connections. It is as easy not to do as it is to do. You need to make an effort.

My suggestion is to only endorse your connections for the skills and expertise that you have experience with or have seen proof of. Don't just give blanket endorsements across a bundle of their skills unless, of course, you believe them to be applicable to your experience.

Look at the top three to five skills your connection has listed on their profile and consider adding your endorsements there. Typically, LinkedIn members are trying to build up their top ten skills by collecting endorsements for them. Getting endorsed for your top skills and expertise can help you get found in relevant LinkedIn searches for those skills!

The ability to write recommendations for your connections is still available on LinkedIn but is no longer as widely utilized. Giving a public, written recommendation of one of your connections is still very meaningful. I do recommend giving recommendations selectively.

Both endorsements and recommendations are a form of giving and thus a form of smart networking.

Connect Online and Offline Experiences

LinkedIn has greatly accelerated our online networking opportunities. When combined with offline networking, the online experience becomes even more powerful. Meeting people in person will solidify an online relationship.

This can also work the other way around. I attended a conference of female entrepreneurs and met many great women there with whom I wanted to keep in touch. I collected business cards (they have e-mail addresses listed) and contact information for the women I met and sent them invitations to connect on LinkedIn as soon as the conference ended.

Now I'm able to keep those relationships moving forward through my online networking activities.

Make it a point to attend relevant conferences and events in your industry and community.

When you are preparing to go to a conference or event, conduct a search of your 1st-degree connections to see who lives in the city you are visiting. You can easily pull together a small group meet-up or dinner with these connections.

Also, determine who in your network might be attending certain events and start engaging with them ahead of time. Many times, I will set up one-on-one meetings with people who are both in and outside of my LinkedIn network.

If you really want to take the offline/online experience to the next level, become a microinfluencer in your community or industry.

John Willding II is a prominent corporate lawyer in Dallas who did just that. He now has one of the most successful and sought-after professional networking events in town. The event is called "Last Tuesdays," and it takes place on the patio of the Ritz Carlton hotel. John significantly grew his event by selectively sending invitations to people on LinkedIn several years ago. He now has over five thousand connections on LinkedIn. His business has been built entirely upon referrals from his signature event.

You don't have to do what John Willding II did, but you could do something like this on a smaller scale by bringing interesting people together who share a common goal or struggle.

For example, you can bring a group of your LinkedIn connections together for a small group dinner, a mastermind meeting, or a local meet-up. It doesn't have to be fancy. You could even start with a virtual meeting. Your intention of connecting others together just needs to be genuine with the goal of adding value to those who attend.

Connecting the online experience and offline experience is the most powerful networking combination today. This type of networking is very powerful, allowing you to position yourself as a leader and an influencer!

Stay Informed About Your LinkedIn Network

Did you know you can control the types and frequency of e-mails that LinkedIn sends you? There are many nuggets to be found in these e-mails that can create networking opportunities. I set up a filter in my e-mail inbox to capture all of these e-mails where I can quickly scan through them.

To update your LinkedIn e-mail types and frequency, go to "Privacy & Settings" under your account. Under the "Communications" tab, you will see the option "E-mail Frequency." Review the e-mail frequency you have set up for messages from other members, updates and news, group digests, notifications (engagement with your LinkedIn activity), and messages from LinkedIn.

I recommend choosing the "daily e-mail digest" for most of these so that you can stay on top of what's happening with your network and act in a timely fashion (it helps to set up that LinkedIn filter in your e-mail inbox). For group digests, you might opt to receive a daily digest from your top three to five groups and a weekly digest from the others.

Exporting and Leveraging Your LinkedIn Data

Within your LinkedIn account settings, you can request a complete archive of all of your LinkedIn data. Once you click the link to do so, it will take up to seventy-two hours for you to receive it. This is an enormous, comprehensive file.

There is a lot of valuable information in this archive file, and I do recommend requesting and reviewing this data from time to time. However, for the purposes of gathering network intelligence about your 1st-degree connections, I recommend exporting your LinkedIn connections instead. It is much quicker.

Under the "Connections" tab from your LinkedIn homepage, you will find an option to export all of your connections. Within this file, you will have a list of first and last names, e-mail addresses, titles, and companies.

Not only can you organize and sort your connections, but also you can utilize your data outside of LinkedIn to learn more about your connections. You can import your connections list into your CRM, for example, or upload it to other social networks where you can find and follow or friend your connections on platforms like Twitter and Facebook.

You could also potentially upload your connections list to Facebook and create a custom audience for targeting your Facebook ads too.

I do not recommend adding your LinkedIn connections to your e-mail marketing list. This is not a good idea for many reasons. Not only is it a poor business practice to start sending unsolicited e-mails to your connections, but it is something they did not willingly opt-in to receive.

If you want to add your 1st-degree connections to your e-mail list, ask for their permission using personalized LinkedIn messages instead.

Network On the Go

This chapter also deserves a mention about the LinkedIn mobile apps. Both the primary LinkedIn app and the *Connected* app can save you significant time by allowing you to network on the go. Check in with these apps when you have idle time throughout your day-to-day life. Again, over 50 percent of LinkedIn traffic comes from mobile. Mobile is the future for professional networking!

The benefits of networking smarter on LinkedIn are substantial, from saving time and energy to actually making a real difference in the lives of your connections. Who you know is definitely important, but how you treat those individuals and what you do for them makes all the difference.

Now that you've learned how to network smarter, let's take it a step further and go one-to-one with your connections.

Chapter 5

RULE #5: Go One-to-One

> *Leadership happens in conversations.*
>
> - Carol and Jack Weber

Remember a time before social networks when we couldn't just blast out our ideas to thousands of people across the world with the click of a button?

Before social media, we had e-mail and, of course, the telephone.

In the age of social media, we connect with people through the click of a button...without *really* connecting with them. We accumulate online friends, followers, fans, and connections, and we interact with each other on these social platforms. However, this is very different than having authentic, one-to-one conversations with our connections.

The irony is that social media platforms like LinkedIn have made it very easy to engage one-to-one with those we are connected to. Most people just don't take the time to do so. Social messaging platforms are becoming extended e-mail inboxes, and these new inboxes are not overly saturated with promotional messages (yet).

It is the authentic one-to-one conversations that build trusted relationships with the people in your professional network.

> *Leadership happens in conversations.*
> *Influence happens in conversations.*
> *Relationships happen in conversations.*

Engaging the members of your LinkedIn network in one-to-one conversations on LinkedIn can build your personal influence and grow your business more than anything else you can do. Activities such as posting status updates and publishing content on LinkedIn are still important for building your credibility and influence, but nothing is as powerful as communicating at the individual level.

The only way to personalize your communications on LinkedIn is through one-to-one messaging. The key is learning how to use LinkedIn's messaging tools professionally and effectively.

LinkedIn's Modernized Messaging Platform

LinkedIn's messaging platform has been much improved to allow for a more modern user experience when communicating one-to-one. This is great news for the one-to-one strategy discussed in this chapter!

The updated messaging experience has a chat-like style with threaded conversations. You can attach documents and photos, and you can also add 'stickers' to your messages.

You can access the messaging platform from your desktop, as well as the mobile app for communicating on the go (if you don't have access yet, you will).

As this modern messaging platform becomes more widely used, LinkedIn messages will have much greater visibility and response rates rather than being buried in e-mail inboxes.

Make sure to familiarize yourself with the LinkedIn's messaging tools as they evolve.

The Four Types of LinkedIn Messages

There are four types of messages you can send to LinkedIn members that vary, based on your network and account level.

1) Personalized Invitations to Connect

The benefit to sending these invitations to connect with other LinkedIn members is the fact that you can *personalize* them. As we've previously discussed, personalized LinkedIn invitations are more likely to be accepted and to initiate conversations.

You should send a personalized invitation to connect whenever possible. In some cases, it won't be possible, even if you know the person you are trying to connect with. When you send too many invitations to connect that don't get accepted, your LinkedIn account could get flagged or suspended, so be careful.

2) Messages to 1st-Degree Connections

Personalized messages to your 1st-degree connections are by far the type of message you want to take the most advantage of when initiating one-to-one dialogue on LinkedIn.

You can send private, personalized messages to any of your 1st-degree connections at any time. The best way to start a one-to-one conversation with a LinkedIn member is to invite them into your 1st-degree network!

LinkedIn also allows you to send the exact *same* message to up to fifty of your 1st-degree connections at one time. There are only a few cases where this might make sense, and I'll talk about that later in this chapter. When you send the same message out to multiple people (which happens in e-mail marketing all the time), it is possible to use a personalized style of communication. However, it still doesn't have the same effect that a one-to-one message has.

Having exclusive access to communicate directly with your 1st-degree connections on LinkedIn is incredibly valuable. Don't ever abuse the privilege by sending "spammy" marketing messages (these can be flagged by the recipient) to your connections.

I'll give you some ideas on what to say in these types of messages later in this chapter.

3) Messages to Mutual Group Members

At one point in time you could send unlimited messages to mutual LinkedIn group members you were not officially connected to. This is no longer the case. Unfortunately, too many marketers abused this privilege.

Now you can send up to fifteen messages per month to mutual group members across all of your groups, and this includes any of your 1st-degree connections. You will want to use these messages wisely.

Keep in mind that messages to mutual group members are not invitations to connect. You will first want to use these messages to build rapport with mutual group members and let them know that you would like to send an invitation to connect with them on LinkedIn.

If there are no common connection points between you and the group member, you will need to ask for their e-mail address in order to send them a LinkedIn invitation to connect.

4) InMail Messages

LinkedIn InMails give you the ability to send a message to *anyone* on LinkedIn, regardless of whether you are connected. InMail is a paid LinkedIn feature that requires a premium account. Depending on your account level, you have a certain allotment of InMail credits you can use each month.

These credits will accumulate month-to-month, but they expire after ninety days. You can also purchase up to ten additional InMails for $10 each.

Because InMails are paid messages, you will want to make them count! When your messages receive a response back, you will earn the InMail credit back.

When you send an InMail, you have several predefined choices to choose from that give the recipient an idea of what the message is about, such as "consulting offer" or "expertise request." What you select here doesn't matter as much as your subject line, which will show up more prominently.

Send These Quick but Meaningful Messages to Your Connections

Make sure you have your LinkedIn settings configured to receive LinkedIn Updates about your network on a daily basis.

Your LinkedIn Updates e-mail will contain important information about your 1st-degree connections such as birthdays, job changes, work anniversaries, and even mentions of your connections in the news. These updates are time sensitive and provide a unique opportunity to touch base in a personalized way.

It takes very little time to go through this daily e-mail and send a quick (ideally personalized) "happy birthday" or "congratulations" to one of your LinkedIn connections. A simple gesture like this can go a long way toward building a better relationship with a connection.

LinkedIn has a mobile app that will show these important network updates in a way that allows you to quickly go through and send your personalized message to acknowledge or congratulate your connections. The app is called *Connected* and is available on iOS and Android devices.

LinkedIn has said that by using its *Connected* app, you could receive six times as many profile views, seven times as many endorsements, and four times as many InMail messages.

The *Connected* app will also suggest new connections for you and allow you to send a customized invitation. (Make sure to look for the small menu icon to customize your invitation.)

Using the LinkedIn *Connected* mobile app is essential for making meaningful, one-to-one contact. I recommend checking it daily!

Focus on Your MVCs

Who are your MVCs on LinkedIn? Have you identified and segmented them? You may recall reading about MVCs in Rule #4, Network Smarter. These are the people you want to focus the majority of your time on with networking and messaging on LinkedIn.

As a reminder, your MVCs include clients or customers, prospects, decision-makers, professional partners, referral sources, industry leaders and influencers, journalists, and your most loyal advocates. They are your most important connections on LinkedIn. These are the people you want to be in contact with one-to-one on a consistent basis.

Identify who your MVCs are on LinkedIn and tag them "MVC" using LinkedIn's tagging system. That way, it's easy for you to filter through all of your connections and look at just these individuals. Your list of MVCs may evolve over time as well! You will want to continuously upgrade and improve the list.

Ideally, you want to learn everything you can about your MVCs. The more you know about them, the more opportunities you have to serve them in a one-to-one capacity. You will have good ideas and reasons for reaching out to them.

Here is a list of questions to answer about your MVCs:

- What business are they in?
- What do they do and who do they help?
- Who would be an ideal client for them?
- Who could I introduce them to who is also in front of their ideal clients?
- Who do they want or need to know?
- What is their business/work/career background?
- Where have they worked in the past?
- Where do they live?
- What are their hobbies and interests?
- What is their personal family situation?

- What causes are they passionate about?
- What community or charitable organizations are they involved in?
- What is important to them?
- Where else are they active online?

There is a lot of information available online about people these days because of social networks. Do your homework. Connect with your MVCs on other social media networks like Facebook and Twitter. Facebook is a great place to connect because you can learn more about their personal lives and connect on a more personal level. Also, run Google searches on your MVCs to see what you can find.

Your MVCs are the people you want to stay plugged into and keep top of mind. When you have a service mindset with your MVCs and you know what they care about, you can consistently deliver value and help them reach their goals.

I recommend touching base one-to-one with your MVCs monthly or quarterly using LinkedIn's messaging system (you can even set reminders for when to contact each person). Send your MVCs relevant, personalized messages that can further build rapport and develop the relationship.

Here is an example of a message I sent to an MVC leveraging a specific piece of information I learned about through my research:

Hi John (not the person's real name),

How are you? I hope everything is going well! I saw where you recently moved your office. I know how exhausting that can be. From what I can tell it looks like a beautiful space. How is your business going? I'd love to hear about what's working well for you these days! Let's catch up soon. Lunch is on me!

Stephanie

The idea with this message is to set the stage for John and me to speak over the phone or get together for lunch. Notice that I said, "I'd love to hear about what's working well for YOU." I didn't mention my business. It's not about me, and it's not about you either!

Make your one-to-one messages all about the person you are communicating with. Get them to open up to you. Ask questions. This is how you get a response and take a relationship to the next level.

Segment Your LinkedIn Connections

I suggested previously that you tag your MVCs. With LinkedIn's tagging system, you can tag all of your connections. If you have a large network, that might take awhile, but it can be very helpful in organizing your network connections.

LinkedIn does some of the tagging for you. They segment your connections by location, company, and job title, for example.

You can also utilize third-party CRM software to organize your LinkedIn connections. To do this, you would need to export your contacts out of LinkedIn and upload them into your CRM.

Segmenting your connections can come in handy when you need to send a message to many (up to fifty connections at one time). You can quickly filter your connections using one of your tags and send the message to multiple recipients. There aren't many occasions where I would recommend sending these types of messages, as I mentioned previously, but there are some exceptions. I will cover this later in the chapter.

Use LinkedIn's "Relationship" Tab to Keep Track of Contacts

LinkedIn does have a feature for keeping notes and reminders about your 1st-degree connections. You can access and edit this information when you visit someone's profile.

Add notes, set reminders, record how you met, and tag your contacts. You can also use the "Relationship" tab for people who are in your 2ⁿᵈ- and 3ʳᵈ-degree networks, as well as mutual group members! It isn't just for 1ˢᵗ-degree connections.

With the reminders feature, you can choose to set an alert for sometime in the future to be reminded to reach out to your contact. You will handily find the person's contact information right next to the "Relationship" tab. This contact information can be edited as well.

Messages between you and your contact will also be visible here. This is nice, because it allows you to look back at previous communications.

LinkedIn seems to be developing this feature more and more to be like an internal CRM system. Don't worry, all of your notes and information will be kept private in this area. As you spend more time on LinkedIn, it will be nice to have all of the information about your network connections in one place.

Connect with Out-of-Network Members Using InMail

As you now understand, InMails are those messages that you can personalize and send to anyone on LinkedIn. (In order to send InMails, you need a premium LinkedIn account.)

LinkedIn InMails are an extremely valuable tool. They have very high response rates. I have received more benefit from sending InMail messages to influential people I've wanted to connect with than any other form of messaging inside and outside of LinkedIn. Access to LinkedIn InMails alone makes the premium account fee worth it, in my opinion.

In order to make your InMail messages count (and receive a credit back for each one you send), they need to have a strong subject line and compelling message copy.

Keep your subject line short and try to make it intriguing. Get to the point in your message as quickly as possible, but don't be afraid to give a little background. With InMails, you have more room to work with, as opposed to sending a personalized invitation to connect on LinkedIn.

InMails are great for setting up LinkedIn connection opportunities with the people you want to connect with but don't already know. Or perhaps they know who you are but you either haven't yet connected personally or you have no other way to connect with them on LinkedIn.

Sending an InMail before inviting someone to connect with you on LinkedIn will build rapport and set the stage for your invitation.

Weave common connection points into your InMail so that the recipient can relate to you.

For example, I sent an InMail to connect with an influencer in my industry who was out of network. I noticed from his LinkedIn profile that he was a musician and played the guitar. I also happen to be a musician and play the guitar. This was a common connection point that I leveraged in my message to build rapport.

Mentioning mutual "people" connections you have in common with someone is also very effective with InMail. In addition, messages that thoughtfully ask for advice or feedback can work well. Contrary to popular opinion, people love to give their advice. This is especially true when you send a respectful message showing that you clearly value their opinion AND their time.

Can you use InMails for prospecting? Yes, you can, as long as you are thoughtful and targeted with your messages. When your message is professional, personalized, and relevant, you have a much better chance of the recipient being receptive to it. Let me give you some examples.

My sister, Melanie, is a content writer for a certain type of attorney. She has conducted very specific LinkedIn searches to identify exactly the attorneys she is qualified to help. She especially looks for those who might really need her help *now*, and she can determine this by researching the prospect's online presence.

Melanie put together a professional e-mail script to send to each attorney on her list. She personalized each InMail message to the recipient based on what she had learned about the person through her research.

Melanie's message went something like this:

Hi Jane (not the actual name),

I work with attorneys just like you to help them attract the types of clients and cases they specialize in online. I do this by creating compelling content for their websites on a consistent basis. I noticed that you are blogging occasionally and that you are active on LinkedIn as well, which is great!

I'm happy to share some of my work with you and show you how I've helped one of my clients attract more than twenty new inquiries per month if that would be of interest.

Also, do you write your own content or do you outsource this task?

Thank you and I look forward to hearing back from you soon!
Melanie

(Melanie adds a link to her website here, which showcases some of her work.)

Notice how Melanie's message is very specific to the person she is contacting. She thoughtfully shares how she has helped an attorney in a similar situation. She ends the message with a question, and her closing suggests she will receive a response. Remember, in order to get a credit back from LinkedIn for your InMail, the person you send it to has to respond.

If the attorney responds but is not interested in further discussion, Melanie's next step is to let the attorney know she would like to send an invitation to connect on LinkedIn. That way, she can stay visible and provide value to the attorney on an ongoing basis.

It is unbelievable how effective these InMail messaging campaigns can be when they are properly constructed.

When developing these types of InMail campaigns, it is very important that you do your research on the people you are contacting.

I read about a similar InMail campaign in an issue of *Inc. Magazine* awhile back. In this case, a custom fabric maker sought out the founder of a company that makes custom bags. The custom fabric maker's InMail arrived at just the right time. In his message, he asked the founder of the custom bag company if he had any custom-fabric needs.

It just so happened that the founder of the custom bag company had been searching for a partner who could help him make messenger bags that were highly visible at night. The custom fabric maker was not only up for the challenge, but the two became working partners to create the new, innovative messenger bags!

It doesn't matter what industry you are in, you can craft thoughtful and targeted InMail messages to build relationships with *anyone* on LinkedIn, including your ideal clients or customers.

Here is something else to keep in mind: the more influential you become in your industry, market, or niche, the less you have to proactively search for new clients and customers. They will seek you out. Your connections will be referring you to their friends, clients, and colleagues. You will be in the position of receiving messages from people who are interested in working with YOU!

While it is acceptable to contact other professionals on LinkedIn using this InMail messaging tactic, don't ever stop building your personal influence. Ultimately, your influence can do this work for you!

Use LinkedIn Messages to Build Stronger Relationships with Your LinkedIn Connections

Sending individual messages to your 1st-degree connections is easy and free. The greatest benefit of adding someone to your LinkedIn network is having the ability to send him or her a personalized message at any time.

One-to-one messages allow you to connect on a more personal level with members of your 1st-degree network.

You can send personalized messages to ask for advice, invite someone for coffee, or let someone know you are going to be traveling to their city. There are all kinds of ways to go deeper with your existing connections through the LinkedIn messaging system.

Below are several ways you can utilize one-to-one messages with your 1st-degree connections:

- Compliment or congratulate
- Ask for advice or feedback
- Send a relevant resource that shows you are thinking about your connection such as an article about one of their passions, hobbies, or interests
- Make an introduction or referral
- Ask who they recommend for something you need help with
- Invite them for coffee, lunch, cocktails, or dinner
- Invite them to a group breakfast, lunch, or dinner meeting
- Ask if they would like to connect over the phone about a particular subject

I've used every single one of the above in personalized messages to my 1st-degree connections. These are the kinds of messages that engage your connections in one-to-one conversations. Remember, leadership and influence happen in conversations.

If you are sincere and thoughtful with your messages, they will be well received by your connections.

The Exceptions to Sending Bulk Messages to Connections

LinkedIn allows you to send the same e-mail message to up to fifty of your contacts at one time. Each one of your connections would receive the exact same message, which means there is no way to customize or personalize the message on an individual basis.

I generally believe that most people on LinkedIn are not opposed to receiving a message like this if they know you fairly well and your message is professional and relevant.

An example of an acceptable bulk message is when you are traveling to a city where some of your connections live and you want to set up an informal gathering. Another example might be to invite a group of your connections to an event or webinar you are hosting. I also believe it is acceptable to send a content piece that you have developed that can benefit a specific group of your connections.

Make sure you do not allow the recipients to see each other's names or e-mail addresses!

I have also used the bulk-messaging feature to ask for feedback on a project I was thinking about launching. I sent a message to a small group of my connections to tell them about the project and to ask for their feedback. I knew the individuals in this group would give me their honest opinions, and they did.

As long as you use the bulk-messaging feature carefully and don't abuse it, it can be beneficial in certain situations

From One-to-One Messaging to Phone or In-Person Meetings

If you truly want to move a connection to a client, you are most likely going to need to have a phone call or face-to-face meeting with them (including virtual face-to-face). Taking the conversation to the next level is almost always necessary for developing the appropriate level of trust for doing business together.

The good news is, one-to-one LinkedIn messages can accelerate the relationship-building process and get you to this point with someone more quickly.

Leverage LinkedIn messaging to build that necessary rapport around common connection points and shared connections. Use these messages to stay in touch, add value, and introduce your connections to people they should know within your network.

I have found that when you consistently add value through personalized LinkedIn messages, your connections will be much more receptive to getting on the phone with you or meeting with you in person.

In Summary

While most LinkedIn members are either not utilizing or abusing LinkedIn's messaging features, you can make this an area where you stand out.

Start building your personal influence on LinkedIn with one person at a time! Use LinkedIn messages to expand your smart network and network smarter with your connections.

Most importantly, understand that no form of electronic communications can replace face-to-face interaction. What it can do is enhance and strengthen your relationships.

Chapter 6

RULE #6: Get LinkedIn to Groups

Individual commitment to a group effort—that is what makes a team work, a company work, a society work, a civilization work.

-Vince Lombardi

As a college basketball player, I've always been plugged in to teams and groups. There is tremendous value in the collective knowledge of people who share common interests, struggles, and goals. Groups also need leaders. Whether you step up your participation in existing LinkedIn groups you belong to or start your own, it's a chance to be a leader and grow your influence.

LinkedIn groups offer a dynamic experience to connect and converse with other members around common topics, goals, and passions. LinkedIn has also been making an effort to improve the groups experience for its users.

LinkedIn groups are a great opportunity to build rapport, make new connections, provide value, find new prospects, engage with existing clients, and grow your influence.

Creating your own LinkedIn group also has its advantages. When you create your own group, you have much more control over the experience. You put yourself in a leadership position when you are a group owner, which is key to building your personal influence on LinkedIn.

I created a niche LinkedIn group several years ago that today has over thirty-five hundred members. It has been a quality source of new leads for me and continues to attract new members on autopilot. I will be sharing more about how and why to start your own group later in this chapter.

Currently there are over two million groups on LinkedIn. You can find local groups, industry groups, interest-based groups, and everything in between.

How to Find LinkedIn Groups to Join

LinkedIn allows you to join up to fifty groups. The key is to find relevant, *quality* groups that are managed well.

I recommend joining up to the limit of fifty LinkedIn groups. Although you likely won't be able to effectively participate in all fifty groups, there are benefits to joining that many. The main benefit to joining up to fifty groups is that you can see the full LinkedIn profiles of mutual group members, and they can see yours. You also have the ability to message mutual group members on LinkedIn directly (limited to fifteen messages per month) without being officially connected.

Some LinkedIn groups are open and some are closed. With open groups, discussions are indexed by Google (and other search engines) and are discoverable in LinkedIn searches. With closed groups, discussions are hidden. You won't be able to see them unless you join.

Join the LinkedIn groups that align most closely with your *unique marketing opportunities*, where you can connect and engage with the people who fit within your "smart network" parameters (covered in Rule #2).

Also, review the LinkedIn profiles of your existing connections who are clients, prospects, and referral sources to see which groups they belong to. Most LinkedIn members will showcase the groups they belong to on their profiles due to this being a default setting.

I have seen some LinkedIn experts teach that you shouldn't join LinkedIn groups of your industry peers. I strongly disagree with this. Your peers can be some of your greatest online advocates and can help build your influence. You can also find editors and journalists spending time in industry-related groups.

To find relevant LinkedIn groups to join, conduct searches within LinkedIn. Look for industry-related groups, location-based groups, association/organization groups, peer groups, alumni groups, hobby/interest groups, and affinity groups that are a natural fit for you. Enter keywords into LinkedIn search to narrow your search results.

Out of the two million groups on LinkedIn, you will most likely be able to find fifty worth joining. It is important to conduct some due diligence before you submit that request to join.

How to Conduct Due Diligence on a LinkedIn Group

Before you request to join a group, click on the group's "About" tab to learn more. Here you can see the group's profile, owner, and number of members. If it's a public group, you can see the discussions and members of the group. You will be able to see group members who are in your network, whether the group is public or private. With a private group, you will not be able to see any of the discussions.

Keep in mind that the number of group members and the types of discussions taking place don't always tell the full story. Once you identify groups that look interesting, you will want to dig deeper to determine if the group is well managed. A spammy group will be immediately obvious when you look at the discussions, for example. They will be highly promotional.

Look for the frequent presence of the group owner and/or manager within public group discussions as well. This is usually an indication that the group is well managed.

As mentioned, you won't be able to see any discussions within private groups until you become a member. Private groups tend to be better managed than public groups. Also, some LinkedIn groups require that your request to join be preapproved. Typically, I have found that these groups are better managed than groups that allow anyone to join.

Corporate-sponsored LinkedIn groups are typically very high quality and usually have large memberships (Citi "Connect" for Professional Women and "Succeed" Staples Small Business Network are two examples). These groups, along with any official LinkedIn groups, will be marked with an "Official" badge.

Specific industry association groups and some local groups tend to be better managed as well. I've also seen some wonderful "interest" groups that are thriving because the topics of discussion are centered on a specific hobby or interest.

Keep an eye out for suggestions from LinkedIn on which groups might interest you. The key to making LinkedIn groups work is doing your homework and finding the quality groups that are well managed.

Try to build rapport with the group managers of the groups you belong to. This is a good way to earn their trust and respect when you do have valuable content to share.

Add Value and Avoid Self-Promotion in Groups

One of the reasons that the popularity of LinkedIn groups has declined somewhat is because of high spam levels. For a time, members of groups could post links to their own content or offers across multiple groups with the click of a button. This is no longer allowed.

LinkedIn groups are now set up by default to flag promotional posts and send them to the "Promotions" tab. Group managers can review link posts that you share, but most of them opt for the default setting where LinkedIn does the work for them. If you engage in the practice of promoting your content links frequently across your LinkedIn groups, you may get banned from posting and participating altogether.

In the past, you could also share your status updates on LinkedIn simultaneously with any of your groups. This option is also no longer available.

In order to successfully build influence in LinkedIn groups, utilize them in the way they were designed to function. Authentically engage with other group members by participating in group discussions. It's not just the active members who will see your discussions and comments. Many of the non-active group members are receiving e-mail notifications daily or weekly highlighting the active discussions.

With public LinkedIn groups, your discussions and comments will post automatically to your news feed, where your connections can see what you are sharing. Public groups and discussions are also discoverable within LinkedIn search.

Asking good questions to start discussions is hands down one of the most successful ways to engage group members. You will get far more engagement from a discussion initiated with a question than you ever would from posting a link to an article.

Another huge benefit of asking questions to start group discussions is that it is free research. Getting feedback, ideas, and suggestions from your fellow group members can be very helpful. Once I asked the same question across relevant LinkedIn groups about the best resource for earning my continuing education credits I needed for a certification I have. I received over one hundred responses. Best of all, I uncovered a terrific resource for getting my continuing education credits completed very quickly!

When other group members are asking questions, jump in to share your thoughts and feedback. People greatly appreciate hearing suggestions and feedback from group members. Participating in these discussions can also position you as a leader. From time to time, if you have a relevant piece of content to share that could be helpful to the discussion, just make sure it is *educational* and not promotional.

For example, I had written an in-depth article about LinkedIn that was pertinent to a group discussion I was participating in. Within the context of the discussion, I pointed to one of my blog posts mentioning that I had done some further research on the topic that might be helpful. The group members involved in this discussion were very appreciative to have the resource.

When you share content within groups, especially when it is your own, it is all about positioning.

By participating authentically in LinkedIn group discussions, you set the stage for building rapport and trust with members, as well as group managers. Group managers are good people to know, as I will explain shortly! You will also position yourself as a leader, build influence, and grow your network by participating consistently in LinkedIn group discussions.

Sending Messages to Out-of-Network Mutual Group Members

There are two major benefits of joining LinkedIn groups. You can view profiles and send direct messages to any mutual group members, whether you are connected to them on LinkedIn or not. These reasons alone are enough to explore and leverage LinkedIn groups. Many LinkedIn users still belong to groups, even though they are no longer actively participating.

Recently, LinkedIn limited the number of messages you can send to mutual group members to fifteen per month across all groups you belong to. This includes any 1st-degree connections you share group memberships with.

Prior to this rule, you could send unlimited messages to mutual group members. Abusive marketing practices forced LinkedIn to put the new limitation in place. Additionally, this limitation is in keeping with the trend of LinkedIn offering fewer benefits to free members.

I recommend using these fifteen monthly messages to build one-on-one rapport with mutual group members who fit into your "smart network" criteria with the single goal of connecting. Get them in your network. Once you bring someone new into your network, you have a much greater ability to build rapport and influence with them.

When sending a message to a mutual group member, I recommend introducing yourself and mentioning the mutual group membership. After that, dive right in to striking up a conversation about a common interest. More often than not, I use this first message to ask for advice, insight, or feedback.

Here's an example of a message to a mutual group member:

"Hi John,

We are both members of [fill in the blank] group on LinkedIn. I noticed that you attended (name of industry conference) recently. I've been thinking about attending myself! I would love to know what you thought about it the experience and whether or not you would recommend it."

All you want to do with that first message is build some rapport and get the person engaged with you. Later in the messaging thread, after you have thanked the person for their feedback, let them know that you would like to send them an invitation to connect.

If you are blocked from sending an invitation to this person, you will need to ask for their e-mail address. Or, you can review their profile and see if they have an e-mail address listed there.

The key is to use your fifteen monthly group messages wisely. Find mutual group members who could be valuable connections for your network and build rapport with them through these messages.

Partner with Existing Group Owners and Managers

Building relationships with existing group managers is an overlooked opportunity for building your influence within a LinkedIn group.

As mentioned previously, when you first join a group is the best time to connect with the manager initially. You need to be on the group manager's radar and build rapport before you can think about partnering.

Partnering works well when you have a valuable resource that the group manager can utilize to add value to his or her group members. You can find this out in two ways.

First, review popular discussions in the group, including the "Manager's Choice" discussions. Next, send a personalized message to the group manager and ask what key challenges group members struggle with and/or what are they most interested in learning more about.

Ideally, you would already know the answer to these questions because this is your target market and area of expertise. Once you receive a response, tell the group manager you are happy to create or cocreate a complimentary resource (e-book or webinar, for example) to address the biggest struggle or challenge that group members are currently facing.

You could also request to interview a group manager for a blog post or podcast episode on the topic. The group manager would most likely want to share this content with his or her group.

If you build a truly valuable, relevant resource for a group manager, they are likely to promote it to their group members. Many group managers are looking for quality resources to share with their members!

I have worked with a few industry-related group managers to create valuable content for them to share with their members. The group manager was happy to have something of value to share, and I was happy to have the exposure to the group members.

Start Your Own LinkedIn Group

Starting your own LinkedIn group can be a viable strategy for growing your network, your influence, and, ultimately, your business.

One of the greatest benefits of launching your own group is that you immediately put yourself in a position of leadership. Growing and managing a group takes dedication and hard work.

If it were easy, everyone would do it and all LinkedIn groups would be spam-free!

When you step up and commit to developing your own LinkedIn group, members of your group will view you as an influencer in your industry or target market.

If you create a group focused on the people you want to connect with on LinkedIn, you can build up your own LinkedIn network by connecting with your group members. Having a targeted group is a very effective way to grow your network.

You can create many different types of groups on LinkedIn, but there are certain types of groups that work better for the purpose of building your influence and growing your business. These include a geographically based professional networking group, a group that serves your specific target market or niche, a group focused on your subject matter expertise, a group that compliments an event that you run, or a professional alliance group.

Professional alliance groups are those where you can network and discuss industry trends with professionals who also serve your target market or niche without competitive overlap.

I chose to start an industry-based group with members of my target market. My group is very high quality because I've managed it well from the beginning. Now the group has over thirty-five hundred members with new members applying daily. (I'll share some tips on how to preserve the quality of your group later in the chapter).

Through my LinkedIn group, I am able to position myself as a resource and consistently communicate with my members. I can also tap into my group to conduct valuable market research. Over time, my group has served as a key lead-generation source for my business as well.

The goal for starting your own group should never be to overtly market your products and services. Instead, you want to share valuable educational and informational content with your group and engage them in discussions. It is acceptable to share your own content or whatever you deem to be valuable with your own group! It is *your* group, after all.

When you add value and build influence with your group members, you will naturally attract new leads to your business from the group. Group members will learn more about you and how you help your clients over time, and they will already view you as a leader because of your position as the group owner/manager.

Your LinkedIn group can be open or closed. Remember, open groups and discussions are discoverable within LinkedIn searches and search engines. Closed groups can be found in LinkedIn searches as well, but discussions won't be visible. Entire group memberships are searchable within open LinkedIn groups. In closed groups, nonmembers can only see members who belong to the group from their 1st- and 2nd-degree networks.

The benefit of an open group is it can grow much faster than a private group. However, a private LinkedIn group might be a better option if you want to create a more exclusive experience.

If you start your own group, you will need a name for your group, a description, and a logo. Include relevant keywords within your group title and description to help your group get discovered in LinkedIn searches.

Send Direct Messages to Your Group Members

Another major benefit to starting your own group is having the ability to send weekly e-mail messages to your members.

My friend, Jill Konrath, owns a very successful LinkedIn group for sales professionals (Fresh Sales Strategies). She has over fourteen thousand members in her group. Jill consistently finds valuable and "fresh" sales resources for her members and sends them out using the LinkedIn group e-mailing tool. This unique LinkedIn messaging capability allows you to get directly into the e-mail inboxes of your members.

The biggest secret to getting members to open your e-mail announcements is having a compelling subject line!

You can utilize this group e-mail function to send valuable updates, resources, and calls to action directly to your group members (the e-mails can include links). Essentially, this e-mailing feature is just like having an extended e-mail list. The difference is you don't own this e-mail list, nor can you access member e-mail addresses. Still, the e-mail feature is a major benefit to becoming a group owner.

Starting your own LinkedIn group does have significant benefits. Just make sure you are committed to growing and managing your group *before* you launch! It can be a lot of work.

Managing a Successful LinkedIn Group

The ideal group formula I have found is to create a public LinkedIn group, but build in parameters that can help you effectively manage group membership and discussions.

With my group, I have required new members to be preapproved from the very beginning. The benefit of this is a high-quality membership and a discussion experience free of spam. The downside is that once your group becomes more popular and your membership requests pile up, someone (likely you) has to review and approve all of the membership requests. This is well worth the time in the long run.

As a group owner, you can also adjust your group settings to preapprove all posts (including comments), or you can allow certain types of posts to go through without preapproval. I require all posts to be preapproved except for comments by existing group members.

Even with a high-quality group membership, you will still have members who try to promote and market their own content to your members from time to time. Occasionally, a member will slip through your preapproval process and begin marketing to your group.

To maintain the integrity of your group discussions, it is best to require preapproval for everything, which includes discussion submissions, promotions, jobs, and comments. Within my group,

I don't allow any marketing-oriented posts or any posts that are irrelevant to the members. As your group grows, you can add a group manager to help with these tasks.

LinkedIn also allows you to create your own group rules. Unfortunately, most of your members will not read these rules. Because of this, I reiterate a summary version of the rules in my welcome message, which is also customizable. Your new-member welcome message can include a call to action for a valuable resource you offer as well. This is a great opportunity to build your e-mail list.

Managing a LinkedIn group can be time consuming and cumbersome, depending on the size of the group. However, you can appoint additional group managers or moderators to help you as your group grows larger.

One of the primary challenges with managing a group is keeping members engaged so that they will keep coming back to start and participate in discussions. Without any discussions going on, your members will have no reason to engage.

Growing Your Group Membership

When you first launch your group, you will have to go out and recruit new members.

There are a number of ways to promote your group. You can send an invitation through your group manager settings to up to fifty of your 1st-degree connections at a time. You can filter your connections by geography and industry. The downside to this approach is that you cannot customize the invitation with your own words.

I recommend promoting your group to industry influencers and professional alliances who are not competitors. When you ask influencers to join and participate in your group, they will inevitably help you attract new members. As your group grows, give these influencers access to post educational content freely in your group.

You can also promote your group on other social networking sites, to your e-mail list, and to other LinkedIn groups who serve your target market or niche (do this very thoughtfully).

Increasing engagement levels within your group can also help with growing membership if your group is public. Public group discussions and comments show up in the LinkedIn news feeds of your members.

Unless you already have a big following in your industry or can partner with someone who does, growing a quality group is a slow and steady process.

Keeping Up with Your Most Important Groups

There are a couple of ways to keep up with what is happening within the LinkedIn groups you belong to.

First, you can always visit your "Groups" page on LinkedIn to scan and search the latest discussions across all groups. You will also see recommended groups to join.

From this same "Groups" page, you can navigate to any individual group you belong to, comment on recent discussions, or start a new discussion with any of your groups.

Another way to keep up with group discussions is through group digest e-mails that are sent from LinkedIn. Recently, LinkedIn has aggregated group updates into a single e-mail in an effort to reduce the number of e-mails being sent to members. In your LinkedIn "Privacy & Settings" section, you can indicate which groups you want to receive updates from.

You can also visit each group's homepage and click on the "Information & Settings" icon (it looks like a small wheel) to configure your settings group by group. Here, you can select whether or not you will allow the group manager to send you e-mail announcements and allow or disallow mutual group members to message you on LinkedIn. You can also have the group's logo show on your profile.

It is difficult (and probably not realistic) to try to keep up with fifty groups, so choose your top three to five groups to focus on and keep close tabs on those. I have adjusted my settings to receive weekly digests from my favorite groups and for the remaining groups, I visit my LinkedIn "Groups" page once a week or so to scan and search through their discussions.

Many LinkedIn members have decided to curb their participation in LinkedIn groups, so it's a wonderful time for you to do just the opposite. I strongly believe that LinkedIn is improving the groups experience and that it will not disappear. Online discussion forums have been around for years and they are a natural part of professional networking.

Search for high-quality LinkedIn groups to join (new groups are created every day) and make it a point to participate in the groups you currently belong to. You might be surprised at how quickly you can build your personal influence in LinkedIn groups by investing just a few minutes per week!

Chapter 7

RULE #7: Become a Thought Leader

> *The written word is still the fastest way to gather information or realize whether or not something is worth your time.*
>
> - Daniel Roth, executive editor at LinkedIn

Having access to modern-day online publishing tools has allowed anyone with something valuable to say to emerge as a thought leader.

Not everyone cares to be a thought leader. However, if you really want to get ahead in your industry, market, or niche and make a name for yourself, online publishing is the way to accomplish this.

When I started my marketing consulting firm in 2010, I had exactly *zero* clients. I was completely starting over. However, I had learned enough to know that I needed to start publishing my insights to a blog. I started publishing high-quality blog posts on a consistent basis that were laser focused on my ideal clients. It took four months to land my first client, but my credibility and visibility skyrocketed within my specialized niche very quickly.

Precision is a factor when you publish online. Be sure that what you write about is going to be meaningful and valuable to your industry, target market, or niche. At the same time, incorporate your personality into your writing to create that human connection and build your influence.

Outside of your own website or blog (where you should always publish your original content first), the LinkedIn Publishing Platform has become a valuable distribution channel for your thought leadership. The platform is now available to all LinkedIn members (if you don't have access yet, you will).

With this powerful content platform, you have a pretty amazing opportunity to get your content in front of clients, prospects, business advocates, partners, journalists, and influencers who may have never found you otherwise.

I'm going to share with you how to leverage LinkedIn's publishing platform to build your personal influence and attract your ideal clients. It is also a pretty handy tool for staying in front of your existing clients.

Why the LinkedIn Publishing Platform

When the platform initially launched, LinkedIn tapped well-known influencers to contribute their insights. These official Influencers are authors, speakers, entertainers, academic professors, CEOs, and more. The list of official Influencers has grown to approximately five hundred people.

The good news is you don't have to be officially anointed as a LinkedIn Influencer to build your influence on LinkedIn! You can leverage LinkedIn's publishing platform to establish yourself as a thought leader in your industry, market, or niche, starting right now.

Daniel Roth, executive editor at LinkedIn, describes LinkedIn's publishing platform as "your insights, amplified." When interviewed by James Altucher on the *James Altucher Show*, Roth explained, "LinkedIn can provide a *network effect* to your best thinking." When you combine your thought leadership content with your network on LinkedIn, it's a powerful combination.

The LinkedIn Publishing Platform is primarily geared toward longer-form, text-based articles. However, you can also embed images and/or videos into your posts.

Let me cover a few of the major benefits to publishing your content on LinkedIn:

1) Showcase Your Professional Insights

Publishing on LinkedIn is another powerful way to *personalize* your professional brand. Each post you publish is tied to your personal LinkedIn profile. In fact, your most recent posts are showcased very prominently, near the top of your profile!

Anyone who views your LinkedIn profile can check out the posts you have published and become more familiar with who you are, what you know, and how you think.

2) Build Relationships

Content publishing is a form communication. Publishing valuable content on LinkedIn that resonates with your network can play a role in developing relationships. This can happen at scale. You publish your LinkedIn post once, and it continues to communicate your message perpetually. People who are moved or inspired by what you write will reach out to you and engage with you. Many of those individuals will be your ideal clients and advocates for your business.

3) Strengthen Existing Relationships

When you publish on LinkedIn, your posts have the potential to strengthen your positioning with your clients, prospects, professional alliances, business advocates, people in your industry or market, and the media. Your content can reinforce their trust in you.

4) Expand Your Reach

On average, your LinkedIn posts can receive six times the views from people *outside* of your immediate network. This expanded reach happens when LinkedIn members view, like, share, or comment on your posts.

If your reach is expanding on LinkedIn, your network is going to grow as a result. You will you earn more LinkedIn followers who can spread your message (followers include 1st-degree connections, as well as members you are not connected to who can see your posts). You can also see who has viewed your LinkedIn posts and potentially connect with those individuals if it makes sense.

5) Get Found in Online Search

Once you hit the "publish" button on your LinkedIn post, LinkedIn search, as well as Google and other search engines, will index it.

LinkedIn members can currently search published posts using the advanced LinkedIn search feature (you will see "Posts" listed as a search filter). LinkedIn search parameters for published posts can include keywords, time frame, and author.

Currently, only posts from official *LinkedIn Influencers* will show up in your search results. However, I do anticipate that LinkedIn will eventually incorporate posts from members, or at least the most popular posts.

6) Increase Profile Views

Your LinkedIn published posts can generate more profile views. Remember when your profile views increase, good things can happen for your business! I covered the value of profile views in-depth in Rule #1 (Chapter 1).

7) Enhance Your Knowledge

I have lost count of the hours of research I did for writing this book. The one thing I can say is that through my research, I learned so much. Do the research that others aren't willing to do in your industry, market, or niche. When you apply the research process to your LinkedIn publishing, you will also enhance your knowledge! By learning as much as you can about your topic, your LinkedIn posts will stand out.

The benefits of publishing on the LinkedIn platform are too compelling to ignore. If you want to be viewed as a thought leader and build personal influence in your industry, market, or niche, publishing on LinkedIn is a must.

Is the LinkedIn Publishing Platform Right for You?

I don't believe you have to be a journalist or expert writer to succeed with LinkedIn publishing, but I do believe you need to be an average writer. Your articles should be professional, easy to follow, relevant, and interesting. But they don't have to be perfect.

If you are worried that your writing won't be up to par, you can always get help and feedback from others. I know people who hire editors to review their content or have their friends or spouses serve as editors.

Writing is a skill that you can improve, and publishing on LinkedIn can improve your writing. One of the best books I've read that has improved my writing is *Everybody Writes* by Ann Handley. I highly recommend this book if you want to improve your writing! The book is a very practical guide that you can use as a resource every time you sit down to write.

If you don't enjoy writing, there are mobile apps available where you can record your ideas (I recommend having an outline in front of you) and have them transcribed into an article that can then be edited and cleaned up.

To grow your following with your LinkedIn posts, you will want to cover topics that are valuable, interesting, and highly relevant to the members of your network. Knowing your audience and the challenges they face is critical (I will share some ways to determine what to write about later in this chapter).

Ultimately, the high-quality content will rise to the top as it does everywhere else online. There are far fewer content creators in the world than content consumers. The biggest hurdle for most professionals who publish is investing the time and energy to put their work out on a consistent basis.

If you can commit to publishing more than one or two articles on LinkedIn, and you have something important to say that can truly be value-added to your network, go for it. This publishing platform is right for you.

The Value of Building LinkedIn Followers

I mentioned previously that one of the benefits to publishing on LinkedIn is that you can earn *followers*. Your current follower count is prominently displayed near the top of your LinkedIn profile next to the most recent three posts you've published.

Your 1st-degree network is automatically following you (unless they manually unfollow you). Your additional followers are LinkedIn users you are not formally connected with but who have decided they want to see your LinkedIn posts in their news feeds.

If you earn more followers, you will create more visibility and engagement for your LinkedIn posts. The best way to earn more followers is to publish to LinkedIn consistently and share your posts with your network.

A quick tip: if a LinkedIn member sends you an invitation to connect and you would rather not accept, you can always send a message back with a link to your "posts" page on LinkedIn and suggest they follow you instead.

How to Write for LinkedIn

The world already has too much content. It's overwhelming. There is more information than we know what to do with. Yet, people are really thirsting for inspiration and guidance from all of that information. They want to feel excited, validated, motivated, and/or convinced by the content they consume. They want to become smarter, more resourceful, and more productive. Most important, they want to connect with the person behind the content!

Much of the content online these days misses the mark. Informative is good, but inspiring is great.

Write your LinkedIn posts in the first person, as if you are speaking directly to the person one-to-one. This is a very effective tactic for personalizing your content and making a connection with your readers.

Next, think about how you can integrate the three Ps into your articles. If you recall from prior chapters, the three Ps include your **personality**, your **passion** for what you do (or in this case, for the topic), and your unique **perspective** on the topic you are writing about.

Remember, all of the posts you publish on LinkedIn are going to be attached to your *personal* LinkedIn profile. They reflect *your* personal thought leadership! What personal stories, experiences, and lessons can you weave into your LinkedIn posts?

You may find it difficult to get all three Ps into every post you publish, but strive to include at least one of them. The more you can make that human connection with your readers, the more opportunity you have to build influence.

Finding Your Content Voice

What kind of person are you? For example, are you the practical voice of reason? Are you the person who takes the contrarian point of view? Do you like to be on the cutting edge as the first to share new knowledge or insights? Or do you sit back and assimilate what others are saying on the topic first before formulating your ideas? Are you a big-picture person? An idea person? A tactical person? Are you funny or sarcastic, or more on the serious side?

Hopefully you get the idea. We each have our own voice and/or style of communicating. Finding your "content voice" is a process. It takes some thinking and awareness on your part to get clear on this, and it also takes practice. The more you can replicate how you would communicate in person through your content, the better your opportunity to make a meaningful connection with someone who consumes it.

I recommend looking at the content of current LinkedIn Influencers or bloggers that you admire to see examples of content voice. Learn to get comfortable with integrating your voice into your content!

Blend *Authority* and *Authenticity* to Build Your Influence

Sallie Krawcheck is a financial industry executive turned entrepreneur. She is also a well-known, official LinkedIn Influencer. Her forced exit from her last corporate role as the head of a well-known wealth management firm is something that she has candidly written about in her LinkedIn posts.

Krawcheck has also written about being a mother on LinkedIn. What she does very well is personalize her posts. She shares her perspective in every post and typically pairs it with a relevant personal experience.

In one post, for example, she talks about attending her son's graduation and realizing how much she had missed out on his growing up because of her corporate leadership positions. (You can check out Sallie Krawcheck's LinkedIn posts here.)

In order to build personal influence with your LinkedIn posts, you also need to be willing to open up and share your personal experiences. I've published posts like this on LinkedIn, and it's not easy. However, when you let your authentic voice shine through, your readers will feel more connected with you. They will feel like they know you better, and they will begin to like you and trust you as well.

Your Post Headlines Matter

I am someone who never thought much about my headlines. I figured they were just fine. Now I think strategically about my headlines for every post. The bottom line is that headlines do matter significantly. It is your post headline that will be more prominently displayed on your profile and in the LinkedIn news feed.

In a study conducted by LinkedIn and Percolate,[6] 28 percent of the top 250 LinkedIn posts contained the words "Who," "What," "When," "Where," "Why," or "How" in their title. Twenty-seven percent of the top 250 posts contained the pronoun "You" or "Your." List posts also performed well (such as "5 Ways to Improve Your LinkedIn Profile").

There are some great resources that can help you create better headlines. However, the easiest way to get started with improving your headlines is to review popular business blogs and comb through your favorite business magazines. Notice the headlines that make you want to read the actual articles!

Only 20 percent of the people who read headlines actually continue on to read the full article. Make your headlines count.

Publish Your Thought Leadership

LinkedIn is by far the best social platform for positioning yourself as a thought leader in your industry or target market.

Thought leadership is not difficult to earn, nor is it dead, as some believe. It is alive and well, especially online and on the LinkedIn Publishing Platform!

Dorie Clark, author of *Stand Out: How to Come Up with Your Breakthrough Idea and Build a Following Around It*, explains that thought leadership is something you earn by sharing your thoughts and building a following around them.

The LinkedIn Publishing Platform is an ideal place to position yourself as a thought leader. You already have a built-in audience with your LinkedIn network as well.

Don't ever attempt to market and sell your services through your LinkedIn posts. Remember, you want to market your message in a way that adds value to your ideal clients or customers. With LinkedIn, your entire network will not be made up of clients and customers, of course. But ultimately, you want

---

[6] Percolate Blog: "What we found when we analyzed the top 1000 posts on LinkedIn" (https://blog.percolate.com/2015/03/top-1000-posts-linkedin-marketing-analysis/)

your content on LinkedIn to strike a chord with your connections and followers.

Writing insightful long-form posts on LinkedIn that appeal to the professionals in your network does require you to be deeply in tune with them. What are their needs and desires? What are their problems and struggles? What do they desperately need guidance with?

People never forget when you point them in the right direction and give them valuable guidance. This is what thought leaders do. They aren't afraid to take a stand and lead. Publishing your thought leadership on LinkedIn will enhance your credibility and grow your personal influence.

Educate through Your LinkedIn Posts

Teaching through your LinkedIn posts can be very effective.

What can you teach through your LinkedIn posts? What expertise can you share that can help LinkedIn members get smarter, improve, and overcome challenges? Can you weave in a personal story to illustrate your point?

So many content creators are reluctant to give away what they know. They don't want to share their secrets. Doing just the opposite is what works. First of all, don't take for granted that others already have the knowledge that you have. They do not know what you know.

Also, most people don't have the time or energy to do the research and gather all the content available on a particular subject, much less organize it into a logical flow. When you organize knowledge in this way for your ideal clients, you create significant value for them.

As a former high school teacher, I learned how to break down broad subjects into modules, and lessons for each module. You certainly don't have to have teaching experience to teach. Start by making a simple outline for your subject matter. Go from broad to narrow and think about taking someone through an A-to-Z learning process for your topic.

Not only can this help to create a logical flow for your LinkedIn posts, it will also give you a roadmap for what to publish next.

Repurpose Existing Blog Posts (but Don't Replace Your Blog)

The LinkedIn Publishing Platform is actually a blogging platform that lives on LinkedIn. That means LinkedIn owns the content, not you. In order to own your content, you will want to publish it on your blog first and then repurpose your blog posts for LinkedIn.

By doing this, the blog post you publish on your own site has a better chance of outranking the same post on LinkedIn in search engines. I do suggest waiting at least a week before you republish a post from your blog to LinkedIn.

When you repurpose existing blog posts on LinkedIn, I recommend stating at the top of the post where the original post was published (include a link back to your website). You also might want to change up your headline and even some of the text within the post. For example, when I republish a blog post to LinkedIn, I use it as an opportunity to review and improve the post.

You may find that there are topics you want to write about on LinkedIn that are not applicable to your blog. I've written a few original posts that exist only on LinkedIn because the topics didn't necessarily fit with my core blog content.

Another tactic you could experiment with for longer posts is to publish 50–60 percent of your post on LinkedIn and provide a link to read the remainder of the post on your blog where it exists in its entirety.

One idea is to publish a "Part 1" blog post in its entirety on LinkedIn with a link to read "Part 2" on your blog.

Most LinkedIn members are not going to want you to take them outside of LinkedIn to finish reading your article. I am more of a proponent for publishing a blog post in its entirety on LinkedIn rather than breaking it up in this way.

Unless you already have significant traffic coming to your website, it is likely that your LinkedIn posts will get much more visibility and engagement than those on your blog. Utilize the LinkedIn Publishing Platform to grow your visibility, network, and influence.

When you republish blog posts to LinkedIn that you've already worked hard on, you can leverage your time and get the most mileage out of that content.

Important LinkedIn Post Formatting and Frequency Tips

The content that works best on the LinkedIn Publishing Platform is long-form text articles that are insightful, educational, and helpful to your network. The top performing posts tend to be on the longer side, at fifteen hundred words or more. However, I've had 750 word posts do well. Post length is something I recommend testing, but stick with at least a five hundred-word minimum if possible.

It is important to integrate at the very least a primary image for your post. Otherwise, it is difficult to gain visibility in the LinkedIn news feed when the post is shared. Your main post images and titles will also show up on your profile near the top in your "Posts" section. LinkedIn makes it super easy for you to upload a primary image to your post.

You can place images throughout your post. This works well if you are explaining how to do something and you can use screenshots to better illustrate.

Notice how I made use of multiple images in this LinkedIn post: http://bit.ly/1MPgsO7.

You can also *hyperlink* the images within your posts. An example where I have seen this in action is when an author has written a book—they will insert an image of the book's cover within their LinkedIn post and hyperlink it to the actual book page on Amazon.

Keep in mind that you can embed SlideShare presentations and videos from YouTube and Vimeo into your LinkedIn posts!

Break up your post paragraphs and text with subheadings to make them easier to read and scan. This type of formatting makes a big difference for the reader!

At the bottom of your LinkedIn posts, or even throughout the post, you can insert calls to action that lead to a specific and relevant landing page on your website.

For example, at the end of my posts, I offer a free guide and link to the landing page for this guide. For popular posts, these calls to action can lead to a significant number of leads.

Tag your posts with relevant categories. You can choose up to three categories that are provided by LinkedIn to categorize each of your posts. Select categories that accurately describe your post. If possible, find relevant categories that also correspond to LinkedIn Pulse channels. When you choose *LinkedIn Pulse* channel categories, your post could be featured! (I will explain later in the chapter how to get featured by *LinkedIn Pulse*.)

With regard to your LinkedIn publishing frequency, there is really no set standard. A monthly publishing frequency strikes a good balance between being consistently visible and valuable, yet not overbearing. You could also publish twice a month or even once a week. Most importantly, make sure that each post you publish is value-added to your network!

Who Can See Your LinkedIn Posts

The brilliant strategy that LinkedIn has employed with its publishing platform is to tie all posts that you publish to your personal profile.

This means that anyone who views your LinkedIn profile will have access to your published posts.

As you may recall, your three most recent posts are showcased prominently near the top of your LinkedIn profile. If you use a primary image in each of your posts, those images will appear along with your post titles. (Using an image in your posts will make them stand out more on your profile.)

To see your additional posts, someone viewing your profile can click on the "See More" link in this section. They will be taken to a page where all of your posts are displayed as an aggregate collection. In fact, this is your personal *LinkedIn Pulse* page, which is also indexed by search engines.

When you first publish a post on the LinkedIn platform, LinkedIn will immediately share it with all of your followers (which includes your 1st-degree connections). You can also manually share your post on LinkedIn and on other social networks like Twitter and Facebook. Additionally, your 1st-degree connections will receive a LinkedIn notification that you've published a new post.

Your LinkedIn connections, followers, and even out-of-network members can engage with your posts by liking, sharing, or commenting on them. When someone engages with your post, it may be visible to his or her LinkedIn network. This is the LinkedIn *network effect*. Your thought-leadership content can reach beyond your 1st-degree network.

For certain posts that you publish, it might make sense to send the post link directly to other handpicked LinkedIn members. For example, you could publish a post that talks about a particular influencer in your industry and let the person know you've written about them with an InMail message. This could open the door to a valuable new connection.

If one of your posts does get featured on a specific *LinkedIn Pulse* channel, it can potentially be viewed by thousands of LinkedIn members who follow that channel. Your posts may also be featured in the *LinkedIn Pulse* e-mail newsletter that goes out to members who have subscribed.

As you can see, your LinkedIn posts have the ability to become visible in numerous places within and outside of LinkedIn. This is what makes publishing on LinkedIn so valuable for building a following around your thought-leadership content.

How to Promote Your LinkedIn Posts

I recommend promoting your published posts above and beyond what LinkedIn will do for you.

Here are six ways to promote your LinkedIn posts:

1) Share your posts as status updates more than once on LinkedIn. Remember, LinkedIn will share it once for you as soon as you hit "publish," but many of your connections and followers may not see it.
2) Share your LinkedIn posts to your other social networks, such as Twitter and Facebook.
3) Share relevant LinkedIn posts in the context of a discussion within LinkedIn groups. If you want to share your content in LinkedIn groups, keeping members on LinkedIn is a better way to go rather than sending them out to your blog or website. If you own a group, you can share every post you publish with your members.
4) Share relevant posts with individuals you are connected to on LinkedIn whom you know would appreciate the content, such as clients and partners.
5) Share your LinkedIn posts with your own e-mail list.
6) If you have a LinkedIn company page, you can share your post there as a status update and even run a paid LinkedIn ad to promote the post.

Leverage *LinkedIn Pulse*

Posts that are published by LinkedIn Influencers AND all LinkedIn members are aggregated and curated into *LinkedIn Pulse*. If you are not yet familiar with *LinkedIn Pulse*, it is quickly becoming the definitive online news and content resource for professionals everywhere.

There is also a very powerful *Pulse* mobile app that has been rebuilt from the ground up. This mobile app curates content customized for you from news sources and articles published by LinkedIn members and influencers that you follow. This means that your LinkedIn posts will potentially show up to your connections and followers on the *Pulse* mobile app!

Within *LinkedIn Pulse*, published posts that have been curated by LinkedIn's editorial team are showcased across multiple channels. Currently, there are over seventy official channels, and some have millions of followers.

Finding the *LinkedIn Pulse* homepage is a bit challenging. This is currently where it lives: linkedin.com/pulse/discover.

You will definitely want to visit the *LinkedIn Pulse* homepage to review and select all of the channels (and Influencers) you wish to follow.

It is also a good idea to review these channels and the posts within them to better understand the topics that LinkedIn members are interested in reading about. In particular, review those channels that are most relevant to your industry, market, or niche.

Source Topic Ideas from *LinkedIn Pulse*

Study what top LinkedIn Influencers are writing about on LinkedIn. What are the top posts from your favorite influencers or the influencers in your industry? Note the headlines that capture your attention as well.

Study top posts in the *LinkedIn Pulse* channels that you follow. Which topics have received more engagement? Review the comments on those top posts. Many times, comments can reveal questions that may not have been addressed in these top posts. You can learn from these insights and write an even better post.

How to Get Your Posts Featured by *LinkedIn Pulse*

If your LinkedIn post is picked up by the *LinkedIn Pulse* editorial team, it can gain major visibility and potentially go viral.

Although it isn't easy to get featured, it is very possible. In a joint study conducted by Percolate and LinkedIn[7] that analyzed top-performing posts on *LinkedIn Pulse*, more than half of the best-performing posts were written by everyday people!

The best way to get a post featured on *LinkedIn Pulse* is by writing about a topic that corresponds to one of the many *LinkedIn Pulse* channels, and tagging or categorizing the posts using appropriate channel names.

For example, I recently wrote about the topic of my most valuable career mistake and tagged my post with "career management" and "career development." The post was featured by *LinkedIn Pulse* in the "Careers: The Next Level" channel.

If you write a great post that gets featured on a high-profile and heavily populated *LinkedIn Pulse* channel, you can earn significant post visibility, engagement, and reach. Additionally, your post can be republished on LinkedIn partner websites and blogs outside of LinkedIn!

Getting your post featured in *LinkedIn Pulse* is no guarantee that you will see lots of views or engagement. I've had a handful of posts featured with varying performance. It depends on the channel, the topic, the relevancy, and the timing of your post.

LinkedIn Post Analytics

A feature added to the LinkedIn Publishing Platform in 2015 was the ability to view stats for your published posts. You can view your stats on a post-by-post basis. Visit each post individually and click the "View Stats" button.

---

[7] Percolate Blog: "What we found when we analyzed the top 1000 posts on LinkedIn" (https://blog.percolate.com/2015/03/top-1000-posts-linkedin-marketing-analysis/)

This post data shows you the percentage breakdown of the top industries, job titles, locations, and traffic sources of those who have viewed each of your posts. The traffic sources data includes views that have come from outside of LinkedIn.

Your post stats also show you exactly who on LinkedIn has liked, shared, or commented on your posts! There are numerous ways to leverage this information.

For each like you receive, you can visit the profiles of these individuals and send them a thank-you message or invitation to connect. For each post share that you receive, you can click to view the actual share on LinkedIn and publicly thank the person for sharing! You can also see who has commented on your posts and respond accordingly. I recommend responding to as many comments as you can, especially those that are polite.

Review the LinkedIn profiles of the people who have engaged with your posts and consider sending invitations to connect. After all, these are the professionals who were most interested in what you had to say.

To achieve meaningful results through the LinkedIn Publishing Platform, you will want to commit to becoming a true thought leader and publish your insights regularly.

I have seen LinkedIn members get really excited about having access to the LinkedIn Publishing Platform only to stop a few months later. Don't be concerned that there are more than one million publishers on LinkedIn at the time of this writing. That is less than 1 percent of all LinkedIn members, and much of that content is low quality. Also, many people publish one post never to publish again.

If you do commit to publishing on the LinkedIn platform, I do believe you will reap the reward of building your influence, growing your network, and attracting more of your ideal clients. This is your chance to stand out and establish yourself as the thought leader you are!

Conclusion

This brings us to the conclusion of *Linked to Influence*. I am excited for you to put these seven rules into play with your LinkedIn presence, so that you can experience the power of building your personal influence.

LinkedIn represents the most important professional opportunity in history for establishing your credibility, building your influence, and growing your business. Don't wait! Go and tap this vast virtual network for all that it has to offer you. Your brand in the digital age is YOU. It is not your company. Continue to develop that personal side of your brand and keep growing your professional network on LinkedIn, so that you have a solid foundation to build upon for years to come. I promise that you will not regret it. It doesn't matter if you are changing careers, launching a new company, or looking to transition from an established business. LinkedIn can help you accomplish all of your professional goals!

All the best,

Stephanie Sammons

Connect with Me

I enjoy connecting with my readers online. Below are the places you can find me. Make sure to mention that you read my book, *Linked to Influence*!

Website/Blog

www.stephaniesammons.com/linked-to-influence-workbook

LinkedIn

www.linkedin.com/in/stephaniesammons

Facebook

www.facebook.com/stephaniesammons

Twitter

www.twitter.com/stephsammons

Thank You

Thank you for allowing me the opportunity to teach you about how to use LinkedIn to become a top influencer in your market and attract your ideal clients and customers.

If you enjoyed the book and you truly learned from everything I've shared with you, I would certainly appreciate your feedback. The best way to leave your feedback is to write a review of the book on Amazon. Thank you in advance for sharing your thoughts with me!

About the Author

Stephanie Sammons is a corporate renegade turned entrepreneur. She left her 15-year corporate financial services career in the midst of the global financial crisis at the age of 40 to pursue her dream of becoming an entrepreneur.

As an entrepreneur, Stephanie went from being completely 'unknown' in the digital business and marketing industry to emerging as a top thought leader and influencer. She's been named a *Top 30 Marketing Thought Leader* and *Top 25 Social Media Expert* by LinkedIn.

Stephanie's work with entrepreneurs and business owners across the globe combines her high-trust relationship marketing and selling experience with modern digital media and social networking strategies.

Learn more at www.StephanieSammons.com.

16065567R00097

Printed in Great Britain
by Amazon